IF YOU CAN TALK, start on the road to writing, dedicated to demystifying the writing experience. Taking you inside the creative mind, the book offers intimate insights from a variety of professionals—from Woody Allen and Miles Davis to Jackson Pollock and Little Richard. Filled with practical advice, workshop-proven exercises, and easily acquired concrete techniques, you'll learn to:

- "Talk" on paper and *discover* what you want to say
- Develop the discipline to keep your mind and behind from wandering off
- Write about the same things you talk about—even if you only talk to *yourself* about them
- Find the writing voice that's uniquely yours!

☆   ☆   ☆

"Simple, practical, funny—and, I love the quotes!"
—Syd Field, author of *Selling a Screenplay* and *The Screenwriter's Workbook*

"Nothing less than inspirational. This surefire program will radically alter your attitude toward writing—from panic and dread to outright adventure."
—Leo Janos, co-author of *Yeager*

☆

**Please turn this page for
more endorsements for Joel Saltzman and
If You Can Talk, You Can Write...**

"An excellent 'self-help' book for people who are scared to death of writing. Gently guiding you through and around storms of irrational fears and negative, catastrophic thinking, it offers useful wisdom that could otherwise take half a lifetime to learn. It also supports my firm contention that with diligence, time, and the right kinds of effort, just about anyone can be a writer. Not just geniuses, British people, and thoughtful women from the South."
—Mitch Markowitz, screenwriter,
Good Morning Vietnam

"Offers specific, step-by-step instructions for overcoming dreaded writer's block and creating a product from a dream. Unlike some heavy books on the subject, *If You Can Talk, You Can Write* speaks directly from the author to the reader.... This book *will* motivate you."
—Shirley Orechwa Maxey, assistant professor, School of Business, U.S.C.

"Witty and inspiring.... With humor and expertise, Saltzman guides you to the writing table, virtually pushing the seat under you and drawing your pen to the paper. In a short time, you'll go from being a procrastinating, unconfident, wanna-be writer to an energetic, let-it-all-hang-out, honest-to-goodness writer. This book should be titled 'If You Read This Book, You WILL Write'!"
—Irwin Berent and Rod Evans, authors of *Getting Your Words' Worth* and *The Right Words*

☆

"Saltzman's book will put your managers one step
ahead of the crowd."
—Steve Sheiner, president,
Sheiner Direct Marketing and Advertising

'Terrific! A clever survey of American creativity that will
amuse and encourage as it teaches you to cut through
the nonsense and write."
—Robert Dawidoff, professor of history,
The Claremont Graduate School

"Guaranteed to get your keyboard clicking when your
writer's battery runs low. Fresh, funny, outrageous,
inspirational. I wrote 70 pages the same weekend I
read the book!"
—Kathleen Adams, M.A., author of
Journal to the Self **and the forthcoming**
Mightier Than the Sword

"An outstanding, creative resource for
all business writing!"
—Peter B. Hultgren, business development director,
Micro Age, Inc.

"Shows how to write in a clear, conversational style.
His book is direct, clear, and lots of fun."
—Katherine C. McAdams,
assistant professor, College of Journalism,
University of Maryland

more . . .

PRAISE FOR
Joel Saltzman's
UCLA
Writing Course

"The response to this course has been overwhelming. Students consistently report that it's fun and inspirational—just what they need to get them started writing."
—Linda Venis, Ph.D.,
heads The Writers' Program,
UCLA Extension

"Takes the agony out of writing and really gets you going. Where are the other Joel Saltzmans and why aren't they teaching in our public schools?"
—Jane Kaplan, producer,
"Good Morning America"

"A sensible start."
—*Los Angeles Times Magazine*

IF YOU CAN
TALK,
YOU CAN
WRITE

JOEL SALTZMAN

WARNER BOOKS

A Time Warner Company

Grateful acknowledgment is given to reprint from the following:

"Elephant" by Raymond Carver. From *Where I'm Calling From*, Vintage Contemporaries, Random House. Copyright © 1986, 1987, 1988 by Raymond Carver.

Geek Love, by Katherine Dunn, Alfred A. Knopf, Inc. Copyright © 1983, 1988, and 1989 by Katherine Dunn.

From the screenplay *Bull Durham*, by Ron Shelton. Copyright © 1988 Orion Pictures Corporation, All Rights Reserved.

Material from "Ameliorating the Image," Spring 1990
Fighting Knives Magazine, used by permission of the publisher, L.F.P., Inc. Copyright © 1990.

Excerpts from "Some Dreamers of the Golden Dream." From *Slouching Towards Bethlehem* by Joan Didion. Copyright © 1966, 1968 by Joan Didion. Reprinted by permission of Farrar, Straus & Giroux, Inc.

A Yellow Raft in Blue Water by Michael Dorris. Copyright © 1987 by Michael Dorris. Reprinted by permission of Henry Holt and Company, Inc.

I Must Say by Edwin Newman. Copyright © 1988 by Edwin Newman. Reprinted by permission of Warner Books.

If You Can Talk, You Can Write is a registered Service Mark for Joel Saltzman's workshops and services in the field of writing.

Warner Books, Inc., 1271 Avenue of the Americas, New York, NY 10020

W A Time Warner Company

Printed in the United States of America

First Printing: October 1993

10 9 8 7 6 5 4 3

Library of Congress Cataloging-in-Publication Data

Saltzman, Joel.
    If you can talk, you can write / Joel Saltzman.
      p.   cm.
    ISBN 0-446-39507-2
    1. Authorship.   I. Title.
   PN145.S19 1993
   808'.042—dc20   93-4204
                                         CIP

Book design: H. Roberts

To my sister Linda,
who let me steal her typewriter
when I was eleven.

And to Deborah,
who let me steal her heart
when I was older.

CONTENTS

PART TWO
Writing vs. "Talking" on Paper

PART THREE
But What Do I Write About?

PART FOUR
Writing vs. Rewriting
or
Okay, I've Finally Got a First Draft. Now What?

PART FIVE
Rules of the Road

xiv □ Contents

One Last Word

ACKNOWLEDGMENTS

First to be thanked, for letting me publish their work without getting paid for it, are friends and students Linda Allen, Renee Caputo, Carrie Freeman, David Hoffinger, Sara Kaufman, C. R. Robin, Elizabeth Rostand, Ilene Shaw, Mimi Starrett, Justine Weinberg, Linda Wilson and Madeline Wolfe. Congratulations, you can now say you're published.

For inspiration and advice, grateful thanks to Chef Michael Baum, Leo Janos, Angela Rinaldi, Gordon Sander, Harv Zimmel and Francisca Matos, who kept telling me I had a great idea until I finally believed her.

For leading me to various quotes, quips and useful information, gratitude to Mary Camou, Robert Dawidoff, Dana Dovitch, David Freeman, Karen Langsam, Richard Marcus, Charles McCaughn and Dan Stern.

For not hanging up on me when a complete stranger called to pick their brains, gratitude as well to fellow writers A. Scott Berg and Grace Glueck.

For guiding me through some of the legal stuff so I could sleep at night, a sigh of thanks to attorney and sage F. Robert Stein.

For wisdom and support, thanks as well to my agent,

Harvey Klinger, who got me to Warner Books, and to my editor, Collen Kapklein, who got me through it with barely a scratch.

And the ultimate thanks to my students, past and present, for allowing me to go through lots of "blah, blah, blah" till I found the gold.

Joel Saltzman
Los Angeles
1993

INTRODUCTION: FIVE YEARS OF WRITER'S BLOCK

When I first started writing, I was fearless. Zooming down the page, I'd fill it up with whatever crossed my mind—writing fast, furious, with total abandon. Those were great, exciting times, but they would not last forever.

After college, living in New York City, it seemed like everyone was a writer. They were working on novels, writing plays and destined for greatness. Or so I convinced myself. These were *real* writers; I was a fake and it was only a matter of time before they found me out. So I tricked them—dropped out from writing and spent the next five years not writing a word.

It was agony, my personal Dark Ages. There were days when I actually considered throwing my typewriter out the window, and myself right after it.

Finally—and you'll find out how on the first page of Chapter One—I got back to writing. My skin cleared up, my friends stopped avoiding me and I discovered the most important thing I will ever learn about writing:

IT'S EASIER TO WRITE THAN NOT TO WRITE.

This book is about getting you to write—with optimism, enthusiasm, and only occasionally wanting to kill yourself.

It's the life preserver I had to invent on my own.

Part One

From Fear
to
Freedom

1

THE FORTUNE COOKIE
THAT SAVED MY LIFE

One night, still in the throes of agonizing writer's block, I got a fortune cookie that saved my life. My fortune read:

TO AVOID BEING DISAPPOINTED,
MINIMIZE EXPECTATIONS.

Not being a true believer in the Fortune Cookie School of Wisdom, I was about to toss it aside, eat my cookie and never think of it again. But there was something about those words that almost made sense to me.

What if I did lower my expectations—*really* lowered them? What if I said to myself: "I don't care if it makes any sense or not. Whatever's in my head, I'm going to write it down."

Suddenly, it hit me: *That's how I started writing in the first place.* I was eleven years old, banging away at an old Royal typewriter, not a worry in the world.

That night, I started writing again, the same way I'd started out as a kid—just for the hell of it. I was fooling around again, having fun on the page, finger painting with words and ideas. I didn't care how crazy, or wild, or silly it got. It got me going again and that's all that mattered.

It wasn't great writing, but it was writing. The dry spell

was over. Having lowered my expectations, I wasn't disappointed; I was elated.

□

I used to throw things out saying, "This isn't great." It didn't occur to me that it didn't have to be great.

—William Saroyan

□

2

IF AT FIRST
YOU DON'T SUCCEED,
DON'T BE SURPRISED

For some reason everyone thinks, "I *should* know how to write." No one thinks, "I *should* know how to play the piano." But when it comes to writing, "I *should* know how to do it."

What if I told you a story about a man who buys a piano, sits down to play for the very first time and is shocked when he doesn't sound like Arthur Rubinstein?

"I don't understand," he complains. "I've listened to lots of music, I *should* know how to play the piano."

Ridiculous, you say? Yet there you are: Banging away at the typewriter, you're mortified when your work isn't as good as Ernest Hemingway's. Hell, it isn't as good as *Ernest Goes to Camp*.

Worse yet, you start blaming yourself, beating yourself up for not getting it perfect the first time out. Suddenly, hammering away at you is a tiny voice that keeps growing louder, an "inner monologue" that keeps telling you: "I can't do this, I don't know how to write. *I'll never get it right.* I'll lose my job. My house. My family's going to abandon me. I'll starve to death, die in a ditch and no one will even care."

And why are all these terrible things going to happen to you? Because you just tried to write a one-page letter and it "should" be perfect but it's not even close. I've got news for you:

UNLESS YOU'RE A CHILD PRODIGY, YOU WILL HAVE TO WORK AT IT.

In the meantime, try not to "should" on yourself. What you wrote may stink, but you don't.

❑

Most artists I know think their work is terrible; they are perpetually self-doubting and are extremely anxious.
I've heard very few artists whom I know well say, "You've got to come and see this piece; it's great." I usually hear, "This piece is horrible; it's a disaster. Come tell me what to do with it."

—Jennifer Bartlett

❑

3

NOBODY LIKES TO WRITE
(BUT EVERYONE LOVES
TO HAVE WRITTEN)

"I hate writing," says Fran Lebowitz. "I will do anything to avoid it. The only way I could write less is if I was dead."

Strange as it seems, writers love to bitch about writing and they really will do anything to avoid it. They'll check the mail, do the dishes, check the mail again—anything to not have to sit down and actually get to work.

You might say that writing is like going to the gym. Nobody likes going to the gym, but everyone loves the feeling of having *gone* to the gym.

"I feel so much better now."

That's what it feels like to *have* written. You've been "like God in the Book of Genesis," wrote Rollo May, "creating order out of chaos." Now you're pumped up, jazzed, feeling like you're finally in control of the world. You left your doubts at the door and you've got the pages to prove it.

Of course, there's one small catch: In order to *have* written, you will have to write something.

"But you don't understand," says the student. "Writing's such *agony*."

So's making love—if you're doing it wrong.

❑

Writing's not terrible, it's wonderful. . . . I'm not into the agonies of creation.

—Raymond Carver

❑

At three o'clock one morning, Thomas Wolfe was observed by a neighbor as he lumbered down a New York City street chanting, "I wrote ten thousand words today, I wrote ten thousand words today!"

That's forty double-spaced pages. No wonder he couldn't sleep.

4

IF WRITING'S
SO WONDERFUL,
WHAT'S STOPPING ME?

Perfectionism. The "I have to get it right the first time" syndrome.

I know. You want to make it brilliant the first time out. It's a nice idea, but it just doesn't work that way. The way perfectionism works is to tie you up in knots, sending you fleeing from your desk and making you so crazy you can't write a word.

OPTION ONE

If you want to create massive writer's block, insist on being a perfectionist; if you want to snuff out the creative impulse, insist on being a perfectionist; if you want to torture yourself for the rest of your life for never being good enough, insist on being a perfectionist.

OPTION TWO

Insist on *not* being a perfectionist. *Insist on it.*

"But if I'm not a perfectionist, won't that result in sloppy work?"

Not at all. But it *will* give you the freedom to start writing without having a panic attack before the first word even hits the page.

A lot of creative people have learned this crucial lesson, usually by starting out by wanting to "make it perfect." Until one day it suddenly dawns on them: "I'm just starting out here. Who the hell am I to demand perfection of myself!? I don't have a *prayer* of making it perfect!"

In 1965, Bob Dylan wrote: "I have given up at making any attempt at perfection." (Now that's perfect.) Meanwhile, Dylan went on to write and record hundreds of songs, become a songwriting legend and win a Grammy Award for Lifetime Achievement.

"Hmmm. Maybe this letting go of perfectionism isn't such a bad idea after all. It might even get me writing for a change."

A NOT-SO-SECRET FORMULA FOR PROCRASTINATION

Chances are, you've already discovered this award-losing formula for yourself. Maybe you even practice it by not writing every day. But just to clarify things, it works like this:

PERFECTIONISM LEADS TO PARALYSIS, WHICH LEADS TO PROCRASTINATION.

As a victim of *perfectionism* you're constantly telling yourself, "It's writing, so I've got to make it perfect. I've got to watch my grammar, spelling, sentence structure. It's got to be perfect." Unfortunately, this soon results in *paralysis*, the numbing realization that, "I want to make it perfect, but I don't know how to make it perfect!" Next thing you know, it's "I'll see if the mail's here. I'll make some coffee. I'll make some phone calls. I'll . . . I'll . . . I'll *procrastinate* by doing anything that's not writing!"

"But I'm not procrastinating, I'm *trying* to write!"

What you're doing is starting to write, then stopping yourself—sometimes after just a word or two—because it "should" be perfect but it's not even close.

This is a brilliant, foolproof strategy. By refusing to accept anything less than perfection, you've reduced your failure rate to zero percent. Problem is, you've done the same to your success rate.

If living your life as a perfectionist is netting you zero pages a day and driving you up a wall, you can remain a perfectionist and wonder why nothing ever changes, or you can adopt a much saner and more productive point of view:

PROGRESS, NOT PERFECTION

I first encountered this saying when a friend came over wearing it on his T-shirt. (I dragged him to the local copy shop, had him take off his shirt, and we photocopied it on the spot.) This message, based on the teachings of Alcoholics Anonymous, sits in a small frame above my desk and saves my life at least once a day. It reminds me to not even *try* for perfection, because the more I try for it, the less I get done. Instead, I look over my work and ask myself: "Is it better than it was before? Is it any less terrible than it was an hour ago?" If it is, I know I'm making progress—even if it *is* far from perfect.

Remember: No one can make it perfect. You can't. I can't. I don't even want to.

□

"Perfection" is man's ultimate illusion. It simply doesn't exist in the universe. . . . If you are a perfectionist, you are guaranteed to be a loser in whatever you do.
—David Burns, M.D.

□

5

"TALKING" ON PAPER

Have you ever watched a stutterer get hung up on a word? Desperate not to make a mistake, he ties his tongue up in knots. It's as if he's saying to himself, "I'd like to get this word out, but what if it's the *wrong* word? Maybe I shouldn't even risk it."

This is what happens when you try to make it "perfect" at the same time you're trying to get it down on paper. You cancel out every thought and wind up editing yourself into oblivion. There you are, "stuttering" on paper and making yourself miserable in the process. Pretty soon you just can't take it anymore. That's when you give up, make a beeline for the refrigerator and you're back to procrastinating.

So how do you write something without trying to make it "perfect" and editing yourself to death?

You don't "write" it at all. You just start "talking" on paper. Instead of telling yourself, "I want to make it perfect, but I don't know *how* to make it perfect," tell yourself:

"I'm going to 'talk' on paper. And the more I talk, the better chance I have of finding something good. Then I can go back and edit it later—*after* I've said it."

Think of it this way: When you're talking with someone, do you stop every couple of words and say, "No, that's not it"? *Of course not.* You just keep going. Trying this. Trying that. Trying to figure out what the hell you're trying to say in the first place. You're certainly not looking for perfection when you talk, just a little progress.

In contrast, saying to yourself, "Now I'm going to *write* something" is a dangerous state of mind—making you tense, anxious and ready to quit before you even get started. Yet saying, "Now I'm going to *talk* about something" is a very natural thing to do. And it's a lot less threatening.

TRUE STORY

Years ago, long before I'd thought about writing this book, someone at a party asked me, "Why can't I write?" This was not an easy question, and I soon found myself going on and on about not much at all. Finally, after fifteen minutes of blathering like an idiot, I heard myself say, "Look, if you can talk, you can write."

I was stunned. I had never heard these words before and I immediately wrote them down. Having gone "Blah, blah, blah" for a quarter of an hour, I'd suddenly said something interesting.

That said, let me introduce you to the most empowering lesson this book has to offer:

> "Blah, blah, blah. Blah, blah, blah.
> Blah, blah, blah . . . GOLD!"

In other words, the more you "talk" on paper—without stopping to judge or criticize yourself—the better your chances of stumbling onto something good. Then you can go back and polish, or edit, it later—*after* you've found it.

You're like a prospector panning for gold, diligent and methodical, sifting, perhaps, through many pans of sand before you find your first speck of gold.

Meanwhile, you must not grow anxious or lose your patience, yelling: "Sand, sand! I can't stand any more of this lousy sand!" Instead, learn to *expect* the sand. Lots of it. That's just how it goes: Sand, sand, something worth keeping.

☐

It might take me 10 pages of nothing, of terrible writing, and then I'll get a line, and I'll think, "That's what I mean!" What you're doing is hunting for what you mean, what you're trying to say. You don't know when you start.

—Anne Sexton

☐

Freewriting Exercise: "Talking on Paper"

For the next two minutes, start "talking" on paper. Whatever's in your head, write it down. It does not have to be brilliant, or clever, or even make any sense. Your job is to simply keep "talking" on paper, having the freedom to go "Blah, blah, blah," with no expectations for the final result.

It's like a Ouija board or analysis. Just keep "talking." It will take you somewhere.

For example:

"Boy it's hot in here. Stuffy too. Very stuffy. Stuffy! yeah, yeah, yeah. that's what the Beatles would say when they couldn't think of anything. yeah, yeah, yeah. that's me. nothing to say, but it's okay. good morning, good morning. good morning, yeah. yeah. yeah. She loves me, she loves me not, she gives me knots in my stomach when I see her, when I don't see her. I see, you see, we all see the truth of it: I love her and she don't care. No, that's just a line from the song. She *does* care and I do too. I do, I do. We're engaged now, pretty soon I'll be saying, 'I do.'"

Then again, you might end up with something that just seems to ramble on and make no sense at all. That's okay.

Your only goal here is to get your hand moving as quickly as possible, to keep throwing words on the page, no matter what.

Remember: Don't even think of it as "writing." Think of it as "talking on paper." We'll worry about "writing" later.

❏

One must sometimes act quickly and decidedly . . . be so absorbed in it that in a short time something is brought onto the paper that was not there before, so that afterwards one hardly knows how it has been hammered off.
—Vincent Van Gogh

Never correct or rewrite until the whole thing is down. Rewrite in process is usually found to be an excuse for not going on.

—John Steinbeck

❏

FOR THE NEXT TWO MINUTES, STOP READING AND START "TALKING" ON PAPER!

Exercise Feedback: "Student–Teacher Conference"

"Did you notice that your level of anxiety was fairly high before you started but that it *decreased* as you were writing?"

"Yeah, so?"

"Like I said: *It's easier to write than not to write.*"

"But it's just an exercise. How's it going to help me with writing?"

"It got you writing, didn't it?"

"But did I really learn a skill? Something I can apply to regular writing?"

"Take a look at what you've written. Do you have a line or thought on the page you might not have known you had in your head?"

"Maybe."

"And did the exercise get you writing about something even though you didn't think you had anything to write about? Something you could go back to and develop more fully?"

"But what if I *haven't* discovered something new? Doesn't this mean I've failed?"

"It means you've only been at it two minutes so far. *Give yourself a break for a change!*"

Explaining his work process, artist Paul Klee wrote that he takes a "line on a walk, moving freely, without a goal. A walk for a walk's sake."

Think about what happens when you take a dog for a walk. Are you really in control, do you plan it out step-by-step? Or does it soon become a kind of "collaborative" effort, a give and take between the two of you? Are you walking him or is he walking you?

Take a line on a walk. See where it leads you. If you're lucky, it may just develop a mind of its own.

6

IF YOU DON'T KNOW WHAT TO SAY, START SAYING IT

Contrary to popular belief, writers do not say to themselves, "Now that I know what I'm going to write, I'll sit down and write it." Instead, they go along with Henry Miller, who said, "Writing, like life itself, is a voyage of discovery."

It may not be freewriting exactly—you may have *some* idea of what you want to say ("I'd like to write a story about X" or "I need to write a chapter about Y")—but beyond that initial spark, it's pretty much open road, "a voyage of discovery."

Right now, for example, I have no idea how I'm going to continue this thought. I need to *discover* the way—by writing about it, by "saying" what my problem is and listening for an answer, or even a hint of an answer, that just might pop up if I keep "talking" long enough, driving around the page till I find something interesting.

Yes, I like that idea. *Driving around the page.* That's what you're doing on your "voyage of discovery."

Imagine you're on vacation driving through New Mexico. Are you clutching the wheel, yelling, "Where the hell's that scenic pueblo that's supposed to be here?" Or are you driving along, nice and easy, ready to "discover" whatever the road has to offer—even if you *thought* you knew where you were headed in the first place?

"What I enjoy in writing a novel," says Mario Vargas

Llosa, "is to discover the possibilities of a story . . . to discover that something has been pushing me in a direction that I could not expect when I started."

Now, to be fair, you may find yourself on a journey that's not exactly loaded with possibilities. Even on the best of voyages there will be dull, anxious times. Times when you ask yourself: "Is it worth going on or have I hit a dead end?"

In 1960, Ella Fitzgerald was singing "Mack the Knife" to a crowd in Berlin. It was the first time she had sung the song and she started to forget the lyrics. About to hit a dead end, her choice was clear: Do I stop and apologize, admit that I have no idea where I'm headed, or do I keep going and try to make the best of things?

Ella kept going, making up new words as she went along. They rhymed and fit the music, and her performance was a tour de force. Fortunately, the show was being recorded and a record was released later that year. As a reward for her bravery, Ella's recording of "Mack the Knife" won her a Grammy Award for Best Female Vocal Performance.

See what can happen when you don't give up at the first sign of trouble, when you let yourself go on a "voyage of discovery"?

Remember: If you don't know what to say, start saying it; keep "talking" on paper till it starts talking back to you.

❏

I start with a line of dialogue. I have no idea half the time who's speaking or what they're saying. I'll start with that line, and the more dialogue I write, the better I get to know the characters.

—August Wilson

Sometimes I just hear a phrase, and then that phrase suggests the next. Sort of a domino effect that keeps building until I hear a song.

—McCoy Tyner

❏

With *Ragtime*, I was so desperate to write something, I was facing the wall of my study in my house in New Rochelle and so I started to write about the wall.... Then I wrote about the house that was attached to the wall. It was built in 1906, you see, so I thought about the era and what Broadview Avenue looked like then: trolley cars ran along the avenue down at the bottom of the hill; people wore white clothes in the summer to stay cool. Teddy Roosevelt was President. One thing led to another and that's the way the book began, through desperation to those few images.

—E. L. Doctorow, from *Writers at Work: The Paris Review Interviews*

7

NOW I KNOW WHAT
I SHOULD HAVE SAID!

You're at a dinner party when someone makes a thoughtless remark and stomps across your psyche. Humiliated, you wish you could cut him to the quick, but your mind goes blank. So you sit there, stewing in frustration. Driving home, you grow angrier by the minute. "Damn, I wish I'd said something!" Finally, getting undressed, it hits you: *"That's what I should have said."* With rewriting, that's what you *can* say—even if it takes you three days to come up with a "spontaneous" comeback.

Truth is, even the best writers seldom get it right the first time. Actually, that's not quite right. What I "should" have written was: Even the best writers *never* get it right the first time.

Instead, they say to themselves: "Okay, 80 percent of what I've just written is not very good. But 20 percent is. And it's 20 percent *more* than I started out with." As Ernest Hemingway so eloquently put it: "The first draft of anything is shit."

The trick—and this is essential—is to see that a 20 percent (or even a 10 percent) success rate is absolutely par for the course. Even 5 percent can serve as a solid benchmark, pointing you in the right direction. To put the gospel in a nutshell:

WRITING IS REWRITING

Yep, folks, that's all it is. The more whacks you take at it—the more you're willing to work and rework your material—the better it gets. We'll get to a more detailed discussion of rewriting later in the book. For now, keep in mind that a rotten first attempt is a *great* way to start. That's just how it works. You start with stinko, work really hard and, if you're lucky, it gets less stinko as you go.

Remember: The experienced writer says, "This is shit, I'm on my way." The novice says, "This is shit. I'm on my way—to my grave!"

□

I have never thought of myself as a good writer. Anyone who wants reassurance of that should read one of my first drafts. But I'm one of the world's great rewriters.
—James A. Michener

□

Describing the first cut of Woody Allen's *Annie Hall*, film editor Ralph Rosenblum called it a "chaotic collection of bits and pieces that seemed to defy continuity."

"Just for a moment," recalled co-writer Marshall Brickman, "I had a sense of panic: we took a chance, and it didn't work; we will be humiliated; is there any way to stop the project?"

Eventually, about forty-five minutes of film were cut, new scenes were written and *Annie Hall* went on to win four Academy Awards, including Best Screenplay.

□

Thank God the public only sees the finished product.
—Woody Allen

8

SHUT UP, ALREADY, I'M TRYING TO WRITE

Uh-oh.

Sitting down to "talk" on paper, you suddenly realize you're not alone; there's another voice in the room—one that keeps nagging at you, making fun of you for even *trying* to write.

"A lot of people who say they're blocked," says psychotherapist Rachel Ballon, "it's their negative self-talk, which is telling them, 'Oh, look who can write.' It can be the voice of their parents or their teachers, which has now become their own voice."

For myself, every time I write a sentence that starts with the word *and*, I think of Mrs. McGraff, my seventh-grade English teacher, drumming into me: "You cannot start a sentence with the word *and*." In fact, I still cringe a little every time I do start a sentence with the word *and*.

But you know what, Mrs. McGraff? I don't care anymore. *And I'm not taking it back. And you're not sending me to the Principal's office.*[1]

Don't just sit there taking abuse from these people. Tell them: *"Shut up, already, I'm trying to write!"*

---

[1] Dear Mrs. McGraff: Look through the ever-proper *New York Times* one day. You'll find plenty of sentences that start with *and*.

A Foolproof Exercise:
"Getting the Cops Off Your Back"

Make a list of everyone who's in the room with you *not* helping you to write. Include parents, teachers, spouses and supposed friends—anyone whose voice you hear saying: "Oh, look who can write."

Having completed your list, fold it up and stuff in into an envelope. Now take the envelope and remove it from the room; put it in a drawer; keep it out of sight. Do not keep anyone in the room whose only job is to *not* help you write.

Take your cue from Greta Garbo. Tell them: *"I want to be alone."*

"In 1983," says Amy Tan, "a boss of mine told me that writing was my worst skill and I should become an account manager."

Six years later, Amy Tan's first book, *The Joy Luck Club*, became a number-one best-seller.

9

WHY DEAD MEN FLOAT (AND WHAT WE CAN LEARN FROM THEM)

Dead men float because they don't do anything to *prevent* themselves from floating. Same goes for writing. If you don't do anything to *prevent* yourself from writing (like throwing your arms up and screaming, "I can't do this!") chances are you'll do just fine.

Long before Tom Wolfe wrote *The Right Stuff* and *The Bonfire of the Vanities*, he was a journalist struggling to write his first magazine article. He did his research, sat down to write, and became—as he described himself in an interview for the *Paris Review*—"totally blocked.... I just felt I couldn't do it." Finally, says Wolfe, he decided to type up his notes so that "some competent writer" could write the piece.

"I sat down one night and started writing a memorandum to [*Esquire's* managing editor, Byron Dobel] fast as I could, just to get the ordeal over with. It became very much like a letter you would write to a friend in which you're not thinking about style, you're just pouring it all out, and I churned it out all night long, forty typewritten, triple-spaced pages. I turned it in in the morning.... [T]hat afternoon I got a call from him telling me: 'Well, we're knocking the "Dear Byron" off the top of your memo, and we're running the piece.'"

Wolfe's essay, "There Goes [Varoom! Varoom!] That

25

Kandy-Kolored Tangerine-Flake Streamline Baby" appeared in *Esquire* in November 1963, and immediately led to a flurry of magazine assignments.

CONCLUSION

If you want to be a famous writer (or simply finish that memo to your boss) stop saying "I can't" and learn that you can. Just sit back, stick a pencil in your mouth and start "talking" on paper—"not thinking about style...just pouring it all out."

❏

As soon as a word comes from the mouth of the creator, it must be executed. Delay may mean alteration, which is frustration; or the will has been checked in its forward movement; it halts, it hesitates, it reflects, it reasons, and finally it changes its course—this faltering and wavering interferes with the freedom of the artistic mind.

—D. T. Suzuki

❏

POP QUIZ #1
(Ten questions you can't get wrong)

1. If at first you don't succeed, _____.
   a) throw this book off a bridge
   b) throw yourself off a bridge
   c) return this book and demand your money back
   d) don't be surprised

2. Even professional writers _____ get it right the first time.
   a) always
   b) more than always
   c) hardly ever
   d) never

3. Writing is _____.
   a) like throwing spaghetti against the wall
   b) like going to the bathroom
   c) like really cool, man!
   d) rewriting

4. According to Ernest Hemingway, "The first draft of anything is _____."
   a) suitable for framing
   b) something your parents would like
   c) the best it's ever going to be
   d) shit

5. "Blah, blah, blah. Blah, blah, blah. Blah, blah, blah . . . _____!"
   a) Blah
   b) Blue
   c) Red
   d) Gold

6. If you're driven to write, the only thing that's tougher and more anxiety producing than writing is _____.

a) running around the block without any clothes on
b) running for President
c) running for President without any clothes on
d) not writing

7. If you don't know what to say, _____.
a) keep your mouth shut
b) smile slightly and people will think you know something they don't know
c) send a Hallmark greeting card
d) start saying it

8. Bob and Mary both started writing at the same time. Thirty minutes later, their teacher collected their papers and said, "Bob, ninety-five percent of what you've written here is not very good." Bob turned to Mary and said, _____.
a) "Who cares about this crap, anyway? Writing's for sissies."
b) "Say, do you know where I can buy a semiautomatic weapon?"
c) "Hey, I'm doing really good here!"

9. Woody Allen's first version of *Annie Hall* was a "chaotic collection of bits and pieces that seemed to defy continuity." As a result, Woody found himself _____.
a) back in therapy
b) back in therapy
c) back in therapy
d) sharing an Academy Award for Best Screenplay

10. Remember: Writing is _____ on paper. *Simple as that.*
a) best done
b) spitting
c) bleeding
d) talking

Answer Key: 1) d, 2) d, 3) d, 4) d, 5) d, 6) d, 7) d, 8) c, 9) d, 10) d

Part Two

Writing
vs.
"Talking"
on Paper

10

WRITE ONE PARAGRAPH AS BADLY AS POSSIBLE

For their first homework assignment, I ask my students to write one paragraph as badly as possible. Immediately, hands shoot up all over the room.

"What do you mean? How do you want us to make it bad?"

However you want.

As it turns out, most students do quite well at writing badly—especially when they put their minds to it. A favorite ploy is to use a lot of big, complicated words, putting them into long, complicated sentences. Droning on mechanically, they'll make each sentence as dull and stiff as possible. As one student wrote:

> In view of the fact and specifically because life is fair, everything should work out perfectly for everyone without needless and unwarranted efforts to make things equitable beyond the presently existing status quo. Therefore, allow us to disallow any cantankerous, petulant complaining or vociferous, boisterous outbursts on the part of the bilbulous, hard-drinking lower-class. Do I make myself clear?

Hardly.

Ironically, even when *not* trying to write badly, many

beginners fall into the same sort of trap. It's as if they say to themselves: "Because it's 'writing,' I need to make it serious, complicated, impressive-sounding and so on."

They don't *really* believe this, but they don't disbelieve it, either.

So what *is* good writing?

It's writing based on the way we talk—not the way we're "supposed to" write.

Remember: Writing is "talking" on paper. When it's *not* talking, it's "writing." And when it's "writing," it's bad.

❑

If it sounds like writing, I rewrite it.

—*Elmore Leonard*

❑

Reading Exercise: "Find One Good Paragraph"

Choose a favorite book or author (even a good magazine will do) and find one paragraph you particularly admire. Read it over and ask yourself: Is this an example of complicated, highfalutin language? Or does the writer use simple, everyday language, writing—more or less—the way someone talks?

Thank you. I believe you've just proved my point.

"Say precisely what you want to say, as though you were talking directly to the person.... Write as you talk."

Revolutionary words? Maybe so. But they first appeared back in 1924 in Lillian Eichler's *Book of Etiquette*, in a section on letter writing.

1924: They were wearing straw hats, doing the Charleston, and some of the best advice in town was, "Write as you talk." Seems like some ideas just never go out of style.

11

IS THIS GOOD WRITING?

I was innocently shopping for kitchen knives when the salesman asked me what I did for a living. Next thing I knew, he reached below the counter, grabbed an issue of *Fighting Knives* magazine and shoved it into my hand.

"Is this good writing?"

The article he had it opened to had a big banner headline: AMELIORATING THE IMAGE.

"Well," I said, "I'm not *sure* I know what 'ameliorating' means but I can give it a try if you'd like."

By the third or fourth sentence the jury was in. Signing his own death sentence, the author had written:

Strangers and friends repeatedly ask, in these dreadful times of nuclear proliferation, political crisis, moral erosion and social dissatisfaction, just what kind of frivolous or malicious deviant would stockpile [*sic:* collect] hazardous weapons of potentially terrible harm? A conscientious neighbor or committed acquaintance will often condemn these trivial acquisitions and censure the trite maneuverings perpetuated for acquiring specimens amidst universal travails as being "superfluous."

Now I don't like to "censure the trite maneuverings" of a fellow writer, but what I want to know is what kind of person would stockpile *words* like this? The answer, and it fits perfectly, is that the writer is a retired captain of the United States Army, a military man who seems determined to camouflage his meaning with every word.

Apparently, this is a writer who told himself: "Because it's 'writing,' I need to make it serious, complicated, impressive-sounding and so on." (And he did a damn good job of it.) But what if he had simply "talked" on paper, trying to explain his position the same way he'd talk it over with a friend? Forgetting about "writing" as such, he might end up with something like:

> People always ask me how I can go around collecting fighting knives when what we really need is more peace in the world. It's like they're accusing me of being some kind of deviant because I happen to have a hobby they regard as frivolous, or even dangerous.

Compare this approach to the original and ask yourself which version *you'd* prefer to read—the one that sounds like "writing," or the one that sounds like "talking" on paper?

When a writer makes something more complicated than it needs to be, all it does is force the reader to "translate" it into language he can understand. And "translate" is a fair word here, because sometimes it really does seem like it was written in a foreign language.

Take a look at an interoffice memo written by the director of employee relations at a major corporation and see if you can "translate" it into English. (I'm not making this up. My cousin Norman actually found it in his "In" box.) The memo begins:

> Good attendance to include being at work on time is expected as well as a condition of employment.

This is the language of lawyers, bureaucrats and windbags. It may *look* like English but it's Greek to you and me. Surprisingly, the memo continues in fairly simple language:

Our hours of operation are Monday–Friday, 9:00 AM to 5:00 PM. We understand that there will be times when you need to be absent, late, or leave early. When this happens, it is your responsibility to notify your immediate supervisor and inform them as far in advance as possible.

This is the difference between "writing" (*Good attendance to include being at work on time...*) and "talking" on paper. With the first sentence, you can barely translate it; as for the rest, it almost sounds human.

Remember: The more you "talk" on paper, the better they'll listen.

❑

If you work for an institution, whatever your job, whatever your level, be yourself when you write. You will stand out as a real person among the robots.

—William Zinsser

❑

LET YOUR FINGERS DO THE WALKING
(ALL OVER THE PLACE)

Consider the Yellow Pages, an excellent example of forcing you to "translate"—in this case, from everyday English to *their* kind of English. Let's say you needed to rent a car. Instead of looking under "Car Rentals," the Yellow Pages forces you to "translate" it to their own way of thinking—"Automobile Leasing." Or how about that time you needed an exterminator. Did you know to look for one under "Pest Control"? (You did?) Okay, what if you wanted to donate your old sofa to charity; would you be smart enough to look under "Foundations—Educational, Philanthropic, Research, Etc."? (I didn't think so.)

Finally, what if you wanted to find a palm reader to tell you about your future as a writer? Let me warn you, though. Unless you're psychic, you may never think to look under "Spiritual Consultants."

Now that I think about it, maybe the Yellow Pages could use some consultants—like "Real People Who Use Everyday English Instead of That Phone Book Foreign Language Stuff."

12

IT'S MUZAK
TO MY EARS

My neighbor, David, had written an essay for his English class and wanted to know if I would read it. Actually, he thought "Why College Football Stadiums Should Be Abolished" was pretty good just the way it was. But his girlfriend thought he could do better, and she encouraged him to get a "professional" opinion.

He began:

"College football stadiums are a waste of valuable land. Stadiums are built for one reason, to hold football games and the spectators of them. I am going to use the Rose Bowl, located in Pasadena, as my example.

"The UCLA football team plays their home games in Pasadena at the Rose Bowl. The college football season lasts about five months. For the remaining seven months, the stadium is empty. The only exception is a rugby tournament held at the Rose Bowl once a year.

A college football stadium is not a small one . . ."

Neither is David's essay. It drones on like this for another two pages.

"Well, what do you think?"

"It's Muzak to *my* ears."

What happened was instead of "talking it out on paper," David had decided to "write" it instead—not with pompous,

37

complicated language, but with plain, simple English. Real plain. The result was Muzak—dull, listless and completely inoffensive.

What's Muzak? It's music with all the blood and guts taken out, music in which none of the notes are "wrong" but none of them are "right," either. Imagine if Mick Jagger were in an elevator and the Muzak system was playing "Satisfaction." I don't think it would give *him* much satisfaction. Or how about "The Times They Are A-Changin'"—on Muzak? I've heard them both, and it's painful.

TRUE STORY

Years ago, at a cocktail party, someone introduced me to a group of people by saying (as a joke), "This is Joel. His father invented Muzak." Suddenly, everyone within earshot took two psychic steps backward. You could see the fear on their faces. It was if they were thinking, "Here's the guy whose father sucked the life force out of music. If I'm not careful, the same thing could happen to me!"

In a sense, they were right. If you're not careful, if you don't pay attention to the warning signs, you can suck the life force from your writing—just like David did when he sat down and wrote "Why College Football Stadiums Should Be Abolished."

Like any piece of Muzak, there was nothing "wrong" with his essay, but there was nothing "right" about it, either. Yet the *real* tragedy—and this is going to come as a surprise to you—is that David is a bright, funny, semi-interesting guy.

"Then what happened?"

That's what I wanted to know. So I took out a tape recorder and asked him some questions:

"David, what are you trying to say here? Why'd you even write this essay?"

"I had to. It was an assignment."

"Besides that. What are you trying to say here? What's your attitude about it?"

"My attitude? My attitude is it's a waste of land, a waste of money. . . . Here you've got this huge football stadium. *Huge*. And you know how often they use it? Six times a year! Five football games, a rugby tournament. . . . The rest of the year it just sits there."

"What about the flea market?"

"Okay, once a month they have a flea market. So now what does it work out to? Eighteen, maybe twenty days a year? You know what they could use all that land for? They could use it for low-income housing . . . put a park there . . . I mean, we're talking about 600,000 square feet of very valuable land! But then when it's only used for like twenty days a year . . . I mean, they ought to just put a big parking ticket on it and haul it away one night! It's like this huge *dinosaur*! I dunno, maybe just tear the place down and let the wildlife that's still around there at least have some room to enjoy the place!"

"Let's say they can't tear it down, then what?"

"Then they should at least put their heads together and see if they can't find some way of making it so it *does* something. So it's more . . . you know, more productive. Worthwhile. I don't know. Get a bunch of people from the neighborhood together. See what their needs are. Make it *do* something for everyone instead of just sitting there for like three hundred and fifty days a year or whatever."

"That's it? That's what you were trying to say here?"

"You read the essay. Didn't you get it?"

"Not until now I didn't."

Do you hear the music, the rhythm of his language? Is there five, ten, maybe fifteen percent worth saving here? Which do you prefer: David's Muzak (his "writing" an essay) or his off-the-cuff remarks (his *talking* to me) about something he actually seems to care about?

When most people talk, it sounds almost musical—with rhythm, rhyme, highs, lows and a whole range of sounds and textures that keeps it interesting; yet when we write, a lot of us lose that music, leaving us with dull, leaden language—the kind of writing that makes you *not* want to read it.

So how do you get this "music" and put it into your writing?

You don't "get" it, you've *got* it. You've got it when you talk, don't you? The only trick is not to *lose* it when you write. Otherwise, your words just lay there like a three-day-old bologna sandwich because for some reason you took all the excitement from your life and put it on a shelf somewhere while you got down to the so-called "serious and painstaking" task of writing. So now the music's gone, the life's gone, and now that it ain't got that swing all you're serving up to your unsuspecting reader is no-life, no-spice, no-taste airplane food; and if you don't like airplane food, what makes you think your reader will? *It's Muzak on a tray!*

Remember: Writing is music and excitement. It's funny; it's thoughtful; it's communicating; persuading; provoking; debating. Writing was never intended to be—never can be—anything like Muzak. But it *becomes* Muzak the moment you start to think: "Oh, this is 'writing.' Better get serious, here. Real serious. And boring, too."

That'll get you going—all the way to Snoozeville.

As for that "Muzaked" essay of his, maybe David should take his own advice: "Just put a big parking ticket on it and haul it away one night!"

❑

*You have to have room to breathe, to screw around and have
some fun. Maybe it makes for imperfect fiction, but it
provides the writer with a kind of joy, of liberation.*
                                    —Stanley Elkin

It don't mean a thing if it ain't got that swing.
                                    —Duke Ellington

❑

13

PICK A WORD, ANY WORD

Back in college, I had a roommate who was a terrific cook. One night, watching him make a stew, I said, "Michael, I don't know a thing about cooking. Can you teach me?"

"Okay," he said. "But watch very carefully."

Covering his eyes with one hand, he reached for the cabinet door with the other. His eyes still covered, he opened the door, felt his way to the spice rack and grabbed the first jar he could find. He shook the unknown spice into the stew, put it back and repeated the routine with another spice or two. Finally, he closed the door, opened his eyes and said, "Okay, what have we learned so far?"

"Michael, I have no idea."

"What we have learned is that cooking is *freedom*."

Same goes for writing, playing jazz or writing as if it were jazz. Zipping along, banging out your message full of music and rhythm, "Man, you are cooking!"

LET'S GET COOKING

The game here is to pick a word, or subject, and start to freewrite the way you did in Chapter Five. The only difference is that now you have a starting point, a place to "jump" off from and see where it takes you.

For example, sitting in the office right now, I look around, spot a bunch of books piled up on the floor and pick the word *books*. Now all I do is start "talking" on paper, letting *books* guide the way:

> Books. Books. Look at all those books. Look at those books. See Spot. See Spot run. See Spot run on all those books. I didn't do it. Spot did it. What are you blaming me for? You *always* blamed me. I remember when I was a kid and Linda—that's my sister—Linda would yell, "Mom, tell him to get out of my room!" And sometimes, I was in *my* room when she said it."

So you see, it is like jazz, or analysis, because it *will* take you somewhere. All you have to do is "let go" and let it take you where *it* wants to go. Think of it as a blind date with a new word. It might be a bit awkward at first, but eventually you'll find something to talk about.

Consider a student who'd spent the past ten years thinking: "Who am I? What do I have to say?" Given the word *traffic*, she freewrites:

> I hate traffic. Back up on the road going nowhere. Total frustration. Wanting to get somewhere and not being able. The total stress. The struggle of wanting to get somewhere and not being able. Traffic. More traffic. It's stress. It's life. It's wanting to do something and being kept back. All my life it's been traffic. Maybe couched in some other term, in another context, but always the same—someone or something interfering with me, getting what I want. And how many times have I given up what I want just to avoid the struggle? But not now. I'm not giving up now. I'm going to get where I want. I'm going to get there when I said I would. Get moving, you jerks! Get out of my

way, you creeps! I press on my horn. I press again and again. This time it's going to be different. You can't stop me anymore!"

Remember: It all started with a single word—*traffic*. Two minutes later, she'd written a personal manifesto.

❑

A good novel is possible only after one has given up and let go.

—Walker Percy

❑

Guided Freewriting Exercise: "Pick a Word, Any Word"

The instructions are easy. Take out a dictionary and follow chef Michael's example: Close your eyes, open it up and *"Pick a word, any word."* And don't go looking for a "better" word because you can't get inspired by *toaster* or *void*. Whatever you picked, that's what you go with.

Of course, if you pick a word like *neoplasticism* and you have no idea what it means, you are allowed to try again. But if you know what it means, "Tag, you've got *leprosy*." (Though let's hope you don't.)

And no cheating. *If you know what it means, you must go with the word you've got*. Otherwise, you're going to spend the rest of your life searching for the "perfect" word and there's no such thing. Besides, it doesn't really matter where you start; all that matters is that you *start* in the first place.

Again, don't even think of it as writing; think of it as throwing words or ideas on the page, taking whatever's in your head and dumping it out onto the page, going, "Blah, blah, blah," till you find something interesting.

TRUE CONFESSION

In class one day, for a guided freewriting homework assignment, I randomly picked the word *fuselage*. To be honest, I almost went against my own instructions, concerned that it might be too tough a word for my students. Still, I decided to take the plunge. Actually, I decided *they'd* take the plunge.

Meanwhile, since not everyone was sure what it meant, I read the definition: "fuselage *n*.: the body of an airplane, exclusive of the wings, tail assembly and engines."

That didn't help much and there were sour faces all around. But the assignment stuck: "Start with the word *fuselage* and spend five minutes doing *guided freewriting*."

Next week, as they read their results out loud, I was glad we hadn't bailed out, after all. One student started: "Fuselage? What do I know about fuselage? I hear the word and keep thinking about fusilli. You know, the spiral pasta that looks like Shirley Temple's hair."

Another began: "Fuselage. Strip the wings and everything else from a plane and what do you have left? A nice, big shiny bullet. Bullet. Wasn't he Roy Roger's wonder dog who could run as fast as Trigger, the Golden Palomino? That poor dog. They had him running everywhere after that damn horse. Course the only time *our* dog ever ran any place was when you called him for dinner."

Or how about the woman who simply wrote: "Fuselage. The body of a plane. Or maybe my body. Sometimes I wish I could drag my body onto a plane and go. I feel so overwhelmed by everything I have to do. I want to be everything to everyone, but it just doesn't work."

Now keep in mind: Not *everyone* did a bang-up job with *fuselage*. That's just how it goes. You'll do great with some words, not so great with others. If it makes you feel better, one student signed off: "I'm going down in flames on this one! Burn, baby, burn. I am crashing and dying right here on the page!"

By the way, next class he did a great job with *leakage*. Go figure.

EMOTIONAL CHECK-IN

Once you've picked your word, do an emotional check-in. Are you boxing yourself in with anxiety, worried about disaster before you've even gotten started? If that's the case, even a little bit, allow me to introduce a new writing mantra:

> "I'm going to have some fun here.
> I'm going to play around and discover
> some really neat stuff."

It may sound silly, but it works—and just as effectively as all those *negative* messages you've come up with on your own. Who knows? It might just chase some of those heebie-jeebies away.

Now get back to work; "pick a word, any word." *And don't forget your new mantra.*

Starting with the word *shorts*, a beginning writer writes:

"Shorts shorts sports tennis shorts, short pants, walking shorts, running shorts. I have nothing to say about shorts. But shorts, ha! Who cares? Except my stupid ex-fiancé from when I was too young to know any better who used to get all worked up in the springtime springtime when girls/women started wearing shorts again—like it was meant for him. Oh yeah, he's the one who wanted an open relationship, then blamed me for the break-up. What the hell did he expect? I should have known better the way he couldn't keep his cool in the spring. So obvious, so creepy, leering, the young lech. I'm so glad I came to my senses. After we broke up this was the same guy who returned all my letters—at my mother's funeral. And never gave a thought to what a horrible thing that was."

Like I said: All you have to do is "let go" and let it take you where *it* wants to go.

14

BUT WHAT ABOUT GRAMMAR?

Given the assignment, "Write one paragraph as badly as possible," a lot of students—instead of making it wordy and complicated—latch onto grammar, knowing that if they work really hard at it, they can make it sound like they ain't got no education at all.

Why grammar? Because it was beaten into us from an early age that if you want to write you have to know grammar. You have to know your objects from your predicates, avoid the split infinitive and never dangle a participle in the presence of a lady. Yet when it came to talking, it all seemed pretty natural. All you had to do was make sure you didn't say, "Yes, I ain't got no bananas today" and teachers would pretty much leave you alone. Even if you said, "This is the sort of grammar we can't put up with," they'd probably agree; but try *writing* that sentence and you'd wind up with another lecture about dangling participles and the increased risk of standing in the corner with your back to the class.

When we're talking, we rarely worry about grammar or let it stand in the way of getting our point across. Do you ever say to yourself, "Because I don't know if I should use *who* or *whom* I won't even ask the question?" Of course not. But think about *writing* something and it's, *"My God, what if they catch me making a grammatical error?"*

When you're talking, let's assume that 98 percent of the time your grammar's fine and it's just not an issue. As for the 2 percent of time your grammar *is* a problem, half your listeners won't even know. That leaves you with a "perceived grammatical correctness" of 99 percent. All you have to do now is "talk" on paper and your grammar score should be about the same.

Don't get me wrong; I'm not saying grammar isn't important. But I am suggesting you don't *worry* about it right now; because the more you worry about grammar, the less you're going to write.

STILL INSIST ON A GRAMMAR LESSON?

Here it is, the first and the last serious discussion of grammar you'll find in this book:

When do you use *who* and when do you use *whom*? The answer is, "Who cares?" Or, if you prefer, "Whom cares?"

❑

Grammar is a piano I play by ear.

—Joan Didion

❑

Carl Sandburg was rejected by West Point because he failed the test in arithmetic and grammar. The country limped on, and Mr. Sandburg kept writing.

POP QUIZ # 2

(Ten more questions you can't get wrong)

1. According to Walker Percy, "A good novel is possible only after one has given up and _____."
   a) started drinking
   b) eaten everything in sight
   c) yelled at the goldfish for being so incredibly lazy
   d) let go

2. By writing something with lots of big, complicated sentences, you'll force your reader to _____.
   a) go back to college
   b) hire a lawyer
   c) wear tall rubber boots
   d) "translate"

3. In 1924, they were wearing straw hats, doing the Charleston, and some of the best advice in town was, "_____."
   a) Carry a flask
   b) Hide the bottle
   c) Knock three times and say Joe sent you
   d) Write as you talk

4. Writing is talking on paper. When it's *not* talking, it's "writing." And when it's "writing," it's _____.
   a) complicated
   b) impressive-sounding
   c) wrong
   d) all of the above

5. Don't confuse your reader with words like *obfuscate*. If you mean *confuse*, say "_____."
   a) Jab, jab, wok a clock
   b) Jab, jab, wok a *radio*

c) Excuse me, but do you rent flies here?
d) confuse

6. When writing becomes Muzak, there's nothing "wrong" with it, but there's nothing "_____" about it, either.
   a) up
   b) down
   c) left
   d) right

7. According to Duke Ellington, "It don't mean a thing if it ain't got that _____."
   a) ding
   b) dong
   c) custard filling
   d) swing

8. Like cooking, writing requires a good deal of _____.
   a) Worcestershire sauce
   b) battery acid
   c) Alka-Seltzer
   d) freedom

9. Beware the _____.
   a) ides of March
   b) fourth of April
   c) fifth of gin
   d) need to make it "grammatically correct"

10. This is my new writing mantra: "I'm going to have some fun here. I'm going to play around and discover some really neat _____."
    a) nails
    b) snails
    c) puppy dog tails
    d) stuff

Answer Key: 1) d, 2) d, 3) d, 4) d, 5) d, 6) d, 7) d, 8) d, 9) d, 10) d

Part Three

But What Do I Write About?

15

WRITE ABOUT WHAT YOU KNOW

Tell a class of beginning writers to write about something they know and everyone's first reaction is panic.

"But nothing I know about is very interesting."

Sure it is. All you have to do is learn to stop rejecting your thoughts and start writing them down.

EXAMPLE ONE

Mary Cahill, a suburban housewife with two teenagers, once joked that if she were to write a novel, "I would have to write about what I know, and I would have to call it *Carpool*." Accepting the challenge, she sat down and wrote a novel: *Carpool: A Novel of Suburban Frustration*. Nine rejections and one rewrite later, she sold her manuscript to Random House. *Carpool* became a Literary Guild main selection and Viacom bought the rights to turn it into a television movie.

EXAMPLE TWO

Ben Hamper worked as a riveter in a Detroit factory. "I was so bored," he says, "I would think of things and as soon as I released the rivet gun I'd go over to the table and pick up the pen and sit on a box of rivets and write that line down. I'd take it home at night and try to expand on it, although it was hard because there'd be grease all over it. But I started writing just to move the minute hand."

His work paid off. A collection of his essays, *Rivethead: Tales from the Assembly Line,* was published by Warner Books. It became a selection of the Book-of-the-Month Club and Quality Paperback Book Club, and the movie rights were optioned for $100,000, with $400,000 more if the movie is made.

EXAMPLE THREE

Growing up in a Long Island suburb, I used to say that if I had to write a book about my childhood, I could polish it off in one sentence: "I sat on the curb and watched my ice cream melt." Clearly there was nothing to write about here. If you turned it into a TV show, you wouldn't get canceled after six weeks, you'd get canceled after six seconds. Who'd want to watch a show about some disaffected kid growing up in suburbia? Nobody, that's who. Until Carol Black and Neal Marlens came along and wrote a show called "The Wonder Years."

This is what happens when you get an idea, mull it over for about ten seconds and reject it out of hand because you tell yourself it's not good enough, or original enough, or because you just can't think of anything to say about it.

"Who could be more boring than me?" you ask. And you don't even have to think about the answer. Or to put it another way: "If it interests me, why would anyone want to read it?"

When Ben Hamper was first encouraged to write about working as a riveter, he shot back: "Write about working in the factory? Who'd wanna know anything about *that* kind of shit?"

Sound familiar?

What's needed is entitlement, the firm belief that:

IF IT INTERESTS ME, IT WILL INTEREST OTHERS.

In David Rosenberg's aptly titled book *The Movie That Changed My Life*, writer Amy Hempel recalls that when she saw Robert Altman's *3 Women*: "It did *define* a kind of life, not so unlike mine at the time I first saw it. . . . I would not have thought of these people, including myself, as having stories anyone else would want to know. The literary equivalent was reading Mary Robinson's first collection of stories, *Days,* which was published at about the same time. From there, it was a short leap to the realization that what I knew, but didn't think of as being valuable, was. That realization was entitlement, and that enabled me to begin to write. And *that* changed my life. That is, it *gave* me one."

Want to know a dirty little secret? Ninety-nine percent of all novels start with something autobiographical—people telling their own story but changing the names to protect the guilty. "In all my writing," confessed Isaac Bashevis Singer, "I tell the story of my life, over and over again."

"But my life's so boring," pouted Amanda from the front row. "I have nothing to write about."

"What do you do for a living?"

"I'm a masseuse."

I paused for effect, knowing I was about to go in for the kill. "Tell me something: Do your clients talk to you about what's going on in their lives?"

"Oh, all the time."

"And how many clients do you have?"

"Twenty. Maybe thirty."

"Don't keep a notebook—keep *thirty* notebooks!"

True, not everyone's life is as "boring" and devoid of experience as Amanda's. But it's probably at *least* as interesting as driving rivets or driving around the suburbs. *If Ben*

Hamper and Mary Cahill can write about their lives, so can you.

"But I could never write a whole *book*."

Then start with the small stuff, like overflowing cesspools or the horrors of looking as bad as your passport photo.

"But that's so ordinary."

Erma Bombeck didn't think so. Instead, she said to herself: "If it interests me, it *will* interest others." Maybe that's why she's been a syndicated columnist since 1965 and has published more than a dozen books along the way.

"But my life really *is* boring."

Okay, let's say your life *is* really boring—so boring that all you're doing is watching TV. If you were Bruce Springsteen, you'd write a song about it and call it "Fifty-Seven Channels (And Nothin' On)." Or you could sit back, chug another beer and say to yourself: "My life is so boring, I have nothing to write about."

If you're not a Springsteen fan, maybe Kierkegaard's more your style. Never known for being a "happy guy" exactly, he wrote a book called *Fear and Trembling*, and another, *The Sickness unto Death*. And he wasn't talking about a hangover; he was talking about his whole life. But at least he wrote about it.

Look at it this way: By writing about what *you* know— what *you've* lived through—you suddenly have the inside track on telling the story better than anyone.

"What you saw on stage is 90 percent true. It's our life stories." So reflected co-author and first-time writer Nicholas Dante on the opening night for *A Chorus Line*. The show went on to win a Pulitzer Prize and a Tony Award for Best Musical, and it became the longest-running show in Broadway history.

From assembly-line blues to chorus-line blues, it's all part of the human experience. By writing about what's personal, you'll be hitting on universal themes and concerns without even trying. As George Bernard Shaw so wisely observed: "The man who writes about himself and his own time is the only man who writes about all people and all time."

Remember: Stop rejecting your thoughts and start writing them down. If it interests you, it *will* interest others.

❏

I decided that I would write one story about each thing that I knew about. I was trying to do this all the time I was writing, and it was good and severe discipline.
—Ernest Hemingway

I wrote about schools because half of the young people go to school. And I wrote about cars. Half of the people have cars. And mostly all the people, if they're not now, they'll soon be in love. . . . So I wrote about all three and I think it hit a pretty good group of the people.
—Chuck Berry

In every work of genius we recognize our own rejected thoughts.
—Goethe

❏

Writing Exercise:
Don't Just Talk About It, Write About It

Whatever you talk about can be great source material for what you write about. This may sound overly simplistic, but it's a valuable lesson: Writers write about the same things they talk about.

Give it a try. On the top of a your paper write, "Last Week, I Talked to My Friends About _____." Make your list as long as possible, racking your brain to remember everything you talked about, even if it seems completely ordinary. That's what you're looking for—run-of-the-mill, daily subjects: cleaning house, going to the gym, not going to the gym, that sort of thing.

Having completed your list, now go back and choose a topic that sparks your interest; or choose a topic that *doesn't* spark your interest. One student's list included "watching TV"—hardly an inspiring subject. But that's what she started with, "watching TV." From there she began to reminisce, writing about coming home from school and how she and her sister would plop down on the couch and watch TV, drifting off into a nap as the house filled with the smell of dinner being cooked. Finally, she writes:

> Now there's no smell of dinner at the end of the day unless I'm carrying in take-out food. And God knows I could use a nap after a day at work. But that TV. The drone of that TV is the one thing that has remained constant. Maybe those bits and pieces of TV chatter as I eat, clean and pay bills tether me to an easier time.

Not bad, considering she started with "watching TV."

Maybe you've talked to friends about the trauma of a job interview or the trauma of not having one, your father's heart transplant or your boss's hair transplant. Whatever it is, start "talking" on paper about the everyday things you've been talking about. Discover that the so-called "ordinary" really can be extraordinary.

THE ARTICLE THEY DIDN'T PUBLISH
(AND THE ONE THEY DID)

Reading from his homework assignment, another student announced: "Last week I talked to friends about how grateful I was to be unemployed." Continuing to "talk" on paper, Stewart found himself writing a tongue-in-cheek guide for the newly unemployed— advising them on how to live in their bathrobe, gargle with beer and eat nothing but Oreos. We were laughing out loud. We told Stewart it was a great idea and encouraged him to shape it into an article; but Stewart knew better. Assuring us that it was a "stupid idea," he went back to his Oreos and that was that.

Two months later, a similar story appeared in the *Los Angeles Times,* though it wasn't Stewart's and it wasn't as funny.

Did someone rip him off?

Stewart ripped himself off. Rejecting his thoughts, he let someone else write them down. Not only did he miss getting published, he missed getting paid.

16

WRITE ABOUT WHAT YOU DON'T KNOW

"Just the facts, ma'am."

These were the bywords of Sgt. Joe Friday on TV's "Dragnet." Imploring citizens to stick to the facts, Sgt. Friday would wrap things up in thirty minutes and still leave time for commercial breaks.

Keep in mind, though, that each week's "facts" were being made up by the show's writers. They might have made it seem like reality, but it certainly wasn't.

As a writer, your job is more or less the same—to take the various "facts" of your life and turn them into well-crafted stories that *seem* like reality. As short-story writer Michael Chabon explains it: "I start with a setting and a character or two from my life. It's like a math problem—you have these givens. But to write an exciting story you have to depart from them."

"But what if it's something that really happened and it really is an exciting story?"

Okay. Maybe there was that time the grizzly bear climbed into the back of your car, or the time Uncle Wally set the house on fire with a waffle iron. But after you shoot your wad of two or three great stories that "really happened," then what do you write about? Face it: If your life's anything like mine, it's just not that interesting. If it were really interesting, you wouldn't be sitting here reading this book—you'd be out somewhere having another great adventure.

What you need to do is start with something you know about, then move to what you *don't* know about. Don't tell us what happened; tell us what *might* have happened. Invent something. Make it up. Make your story interesting and compelling, even if your real life isn't. Whatever you do, do not listen to Sgt. Friday:

DO NOT STICK TO "JUST THE FACTS, MA'AM."

Sticking to "just the facts," you'll find yourself chained to what writer Ralph Lombreglia calls "the tyranny of actuality." Suddenly, just because the actual event wasn't all that interesting, your story won't be, either. "But that's the way it happened" is no excuse for a boring or meandering story. Unless you're a reporter, you're not trying to be 100 percent factual; you're trying to tell a story, and a good one at that.

"So what *do* I do with the facts of my life?"

Hold a mirror up to your life, but *make it a fun-house mirror*. Change the facts. Distort them. Take reality and shape it the way *you* want it to go.

Remember: It doesn't matter if that's the way it "really happened"; all that matters is if it interests the reader.

❑

Some of my stories are about real people. It's funny how when you try to be very accurate, it's boring and there's nothing there. But when you distort the reality, it comes back stronger than before and is often closer to the truth.
—Tatyana Tolstaya

I'm not writing autobiography. It's all subject to change. . . . Whatever seems to suit the work best, that's the direction I'll go in.
—Raymond Carver

❑

Writing Exercise: Fact to Fiction

Choose one topic from your "Last Week, I Talked to Friends About _____" list and start playing loose with the truth. Release yourself from "the tyranny of actuality." Shape it. Expand it. Forget that it "really happened" and make it happen in a new and provocative way.

Let's say you're a secretary and your list included, "Last week I talked to friends about my boss and how much I can't stand him." From there you could write a "factual" story about someone who doesn't like putting up with their boss's crap but lacks the nerve to do anything about it; or you could *stretch* a bit and turn it into the movie *9 to 5*—about a group of secretaries who band together to take revenge on their jerk of a boss.

Or let's say your list included, "Last week, I talked about the road trip I took with my friend." If you wanted, you could write a story about how this and that happened along the way and make it *sort of* interesting; or you could turn up the heat and make it into *Thelma and Louise*. Which story sounds more interesting to you—the one that "really happened" or the one that might have but probably didn't?

By the way, I'm not suggesting that everything you write has to be about women taking revenge. Your story could be as simple as a man taking his wife to dinner. Just try to make it more interesting than your last trip to the local Sizzler.

Extra Credit: "Closet Stories"

Go to your closet and find something that interests you— something that gives you a memory about buying it, wearing it, buying it and not wearing it, whatever. Using this as your starting point, write a story that *starts* with reality, then goes on from there.

Ann Beattie once wrote a story, "Janus," about a woman's love for the "perfect" bowl. Not what you'd consider a *sure-fire* idea, per se, but she did get her story published in the prestigious *New Yorker*, and after that in *The Best Short Stories of 1986*."

"Okay, maybe writing about that old sweater isn't such a bad idea, after all."

17

FRIENDS TO FICTION

"But how can I take people I care about and turn them into fiction?"

"How can you avoid it?"

"But what if my mother, father, sister, brother, lover, ex-lover, spouse, ex-spouse, neighbor, teacher, handyman, garbage man or best friend reads it?"

"You're right. Don't write about anyone or anything you know. Be nice to your friends and family, don't reveal anything about anyone, including yourself, ruffle nobody's feathers and put everyone to sleep."

"But what will they *think* of me?"

"They'll probably think: 'Look at me; I'm so interesting, someone wrote about me.'"

TRUE STORY

A few years ago, a national magazine ran a short story about a friend of mine, an actor. The writer, having been jilted after a tumultuous affair with him, was out for revenge. Changing his name and a few details (so as not to get sued), she roasted the guy, painting a portrait even a mother couldn't love.

Months later, if you went to his house, he'd pull out the magazine and show you the article. That's how outraged he was. "How dare she change my name? If she's going to tear me apart, at least let me get some publicity out of it."

Like I said: In some strange, twisted way, they may even be flattered.

❑

Everyone uses stuff from their life. There is barely an American writer in the last fifty years who has gotten divorced and not written something about it.

—Nora Ephron

If a writer has to rob his mother, he will not hesitate; the "Ode on a Grecian Urn" is worth any number of old ladies.

—William Faulkner

❑

Writing Exercise: "True Things I Could Never Make Public"

Thinking of your friends, neighbors and relatives, make a list of "True Things I Could Never Make Public." Hold nothing back. Whatever you think of, write it down—bad marriages, family squabbles, drinking problems, sexual secrets, problems with the law, problems at work. When you think you're finished, keep going. Make your list as long as possible.

Now take one of your topics and use guided freewriting to expand on it, fictionalizing your subject as much or as little as you'd like. And don't worry about stepping on toes; don't *try* to hurt someone's feelings, but don't try to avoid it, either.

Television writer Jay Tarses (who created "The Days and Nights of Molly Dodd") wrote his first play, *Man in His Underwear*, about a middle-aged man with a rocky marriage who's having an affair with a younger woman. Asked by a *New York Times* reporter if the work was autobiographical, Tarses, fifty-three, replied: "This play I wrote at a period of my life when I was troubled by some things in my marriage. There were some questions that had to be answered. But here's the thing: The person who loves the play more than any other person in the world is my wife. And it's not an easy play for her to watch."

18

WRITE ABOUT WHAT
MATTERS TO YOU

A woman student in her fifties once told me she was going to write an essay about chewing gum.

"Okay," I thought, "knock yourself out."

I admit it, the subject of gum chewing did not exactly send ripples down my spine—until she came back the next week and read her essay.

As a high school teacher, she hated it when students chewed gum in her class. It was just one of those things that, well, sent ripples down her spine. The result was a fiery, angry, passionate plea. Here was a subject she cared about and she wrote the hell out of it.

Think of your writing as a letter to the editor—the world according to You. Use Howard Beale from *Network* as your model. Go to your typewriter and let it rip; tell the world:

> "I'M MAD AS HELL AND I'M NOT
> GOING TO TAKE IT ANYMORE!"

Know that if it matters to you, you're *entitled* to tell people; and that by telling them, "This is the way *I* see things," you do a good and valuable deed. As filmmaker Albert Brooks put it: "If the result of something I do is that

69

someone feels 10 percent less crazy because they see someone else thinking what they're thinking, then I provide a
service."

TRUE STORY

Early on, teaching the course that became the basis for this
book, I was talking about perfectionism and how it had
crippled me as a writer when I got the feeling I wasn't the
only one in the room who was familiar with the problem.

"How many people here would call themselves perfec-
tionists?" I asked.

Almost at once, everyone in the room raised their hand,
telling me, in effect, "If it's been a problem for you, it's a
problem for us." With a flash of insight, I discovered that all I
had to do was talk about what had been my own fears and
insecurities as a writer. If I could do that, honestly and
consistently, I'd be addressing my students' problems with
astonishing accuracy.

Keep in mind: It's not that I'm particularly bright or
have "keen insights" into your struggles as a writer. All I've
been doing—in class, and here in the book—is having the
faith that if some crazy, misguided thought lived in my head,
it may still live in yours.

This is what happens when you write about things you
truly care about, things you're emotionally and psychologically
invested in. Starting with a subject that's *personally* important, not only are you an instant expert, you'll soon find
yourself writing with power and conviction, telling your
reader: "This is the way I see the world, and by the time I'm
done, you're going to see it just like me."

❑

*All I try to do is to write music that feels meaningful to me,
that has commitment and passion behind it. . . . [If] what*

I'm writing about is real, and if there's emotion, then, hey, there'll be somebody who wants to hear it.

—Bruce Springsteen

If there is a magic in story writing . . . [it] seems to lie solely in the aching urge of the writer to convey something he feels important to the reader.

—John Steinbeck

No tears in the writer, no tears in the reader.

—Robert Frost

❑

Guided Freewriting Exercise: "I Believe"

In the movie *Bull Durham,* baseball groupie Annie Savoy (Susan Sarandon) angrily asks Crash Davis (Kevin Costner) what he believes in. He replies:

> I believe in the soul . . . the cock . . . the pussy . . . the small of a woman's back . . . the hanging curve ball . . . high fiber . . . good scotch . . . I believe that the novels of Susan Sontag are self-indulgent, overrated crap. I believe that Lee Harvey Oswald acted alone.[1] I believe there ought to be a constitutional amendment outlawing Astroturf and the designated hitter. I believe in the sweet spot, soft-core pornography, opening your presents Christmas morning rather than Christmas eve, and I believe in long, slow, deep, soft, wet kisses that last three days.

What do I believe? I believe that Crash Davis could write a damn good essay on any one of these subjects. Do I care about Astroturf? Not a lick. Never even thought about it.

---

[1] This was a few years before Mr. Costner appeared in *JFK* and radically changed his point of view.

But if Crash Davis started talking to me about Astroturf, you bet I'd listen. And before he was finished, he'd make me care, too.

Here's your assignment: Take Crash Davis's monologue and read it out loud two or three times. Then use guided freewriting to write your own "I believe" speech. (When you think you're finished, keep going. Make your list as long as possible.) Finally, choose one topic from your "I believe" speech and *expand* on it using guided freewriting.

As a homework assignment, this has proven to be a foolproof exercise. Not only will you generate a long list of things that really do matter to you, you'll have the experience— perhaps for the first time—of writing with conviction, not apology.

◻

A writer's material is what he cares about.

—John Gardner

◻

To give you a sense of what you're looking for (not to mention their sheer entertainment value), presented below are the "Top Ten" from the past year or so. Keep in mind that these are *not* representative samples. Statements like "I believe in cardboard," for example, failed to make the cut, though it did lead to a pretty interesting essay on how "flimsy" a world it would be if we didn't have any.

Anyway, here are some favorites:

• I believe that everybody thinks they make a great spaghetti sauce.

• I believe that most people would rather reveal their deepest, darkest secret on "Oprah" than admit it to the person sitting across from them.

• I believe that movie stars and teachers should swap salaries.

• I believe that no one in life ever had as much fun as those people in the beer commercials.

• I believe that parenting should be a licensed skill: If you don't pass the test, you don't get a kid.

• I believe people should be able to cry anywhere, anytime, for any reason.

• I believe an orgasm is an inexpensive gift and you can never have too many.

• I believe that every family loves to burp at the dinner table but would be horrified if a guest did the same thing.

• I believe in Neil Diamond and also believe that I am some-what cool regardless of the fact.

• After three kids, two divorces, bankruptcy, and a bout with cancer, I believe—wholeheartedly and unequivocally—in me.

19

WRITE ABOUT THINGS YOU'VE RESEARCHED

This is the research process: You start with a bunch of questions, find more questions as you go, and by the time you're finished you have so many answers you could write a book on the subject.

EXAMPLE ONE

A friend of mine once wrote a "how-to" book about camping and hiking. On the back cover, as you might expect, is a photo of the author, wearing a backpack out in the mountains somewhere. But what you wouldn't expect is that the backpack wasn't his; he had to borrow it. And what looks like a scene from Sequoia National Park actually took place in Central Park.

As you may have guessed by now, this self-proclaimed "expert" on hiking and camping had never done either; but he *did* do his research. His book sold well and no one was the wiser.

EXAMPLE TWO

Another friend wrote a successful action adventure film that was released by a major Hollywood studio. The original script featured a number of detailed and dramatic rock-climbing scenes, and one of the things that interested the producer was the writer's obvious knowledge and passion for his subject. But what the producer still doesn't know is that the only climbing this writer ever did was on the shelves of the New York City Public Library, where he learned absolutely everything he knows about pitons, picks, hoists and carabiners.

EXAMPLE THREE

Two reporters had a nagging feeling about a burglary at a local hotel. They did months of research, pursued every lead and wound up revealing a scandal called Watergate. Woodward and Bernstein became national heros and Nixon resigned from office.

See what can happen when you do your research?

Researching your subject, you may not know where you're headed, exactly, but you take it on faith that you'll find something interesting; that one small fact will lead to another; that in looking to solve X you may just find the answer to Y. To paraphrase Henry Miller:

RESEARCH IS A VOYAGE OF DISCOVERY.

What are you looking for? Any little fact or detail that will help you write with authority, convincing the reader—and yourself—you really do know what you're talking about.

Consider an example from Joan Didion, a seasoned writer who clearly understands the value of research. In her essay "Some Dreamers of the Golden Dream" (from *Slouching Towards Bethlehem*), she describes California's San Bernardino Valley in the 1960s as a place "where the divorce rate is double the national average and where one person in every thirty-eight lives in a trailer." This is a dead-bang, tell-it-like-it-is kind of line—the result, perhaps, of sitting in the library for three or four hours, searching for one or two tell-tale facts to give the reader a kind of "snapshot" of the place.

Later in the essay, setting the stage for the kind of night it was on January 11, 1965, Didion writes:

> A woman in Hollywood staged an all-night sit-in on the hood of her car to prevent repossession by a finance company. A seventy-year-old pensioner drove his station wagon at five miles an hour past three Gardena poker parlors and emptied three pistols and a twelve-gauge shotgun through their windows, wounding twenty-nine people. "Many young women become prostitutes just to have enough money to play cards," he explained in a note. Mrs. Nick Adams said she was "not surprised" to hear her husband announce his divorce plans on the Les Crane Show, and, farther north, a sixteen-year-old jumped off the Golden Gate Bridge and lived.

Now before you tell yourself, "I can't write like that," consider where these lines may have come from—not from some writer's *wild imagination*, but from the simple ability of Joan Didion to say to herself: "Think I'll check some newspapers, see what was going on that night."

BUTCH CASSIDY, THE SUNDANCE KID AND EIGHT YEARS OF RESEARCH

In *Adventures in the Screen Trade*, William Goldman discusses the genesis of his Academy Award–winning screenplay, *Butch Cassidy and the Sundance Kid*:

> I first read about Butch and Sundance in the late 1950's, and the story of the two outlaws fascinated me. . . . [T]here

weren't many books about them then, but there were articles and I would seek them out and read them. The more I read, the deeper my fascination became.... Eventually, I did all the research I could bear...so I sat down and wrote the first draft in 1966.

It took four weeks.

When someone asks how long it takes to write a screenplay, I'm never sure what to answer. Because I don't think four weeks is what it took to do *Butch*. For me, eight years is closer to the truth.

Let William Goldman be your role model: Write about things you've researched so well they get under your skin and won't let go. Then work even harder to make your homework pay off. If you're lucky, it could be the difference between *Butch Cassidy and the Sundance Kid* and *The Lone Ranger Meets Godzilla*.

WHAT DO YOU RESEARCH?

Anything.

Oranges. Bark canoes. A farmers market somewhere.

I know. None of these subjects sound particularly interesting. Yet noted writer John McPhee begs to differ. In books like *Oranges, The Survival of the Bark Canoe* and *Giving Good Weight*, McPhee looks at the ordinary and discovers the *extraordinary. Oranges,* for example, was originally going to be a magazine article. But McPhee discovered so much information he turned it into a 149-page book. As a *Christian Science Monitor* reviewer once wrote: "John McPhee ought to be a bore. With a bore's persistence, he seizes a subject, shakes loose a cloud of more detail than we ever imagined we would care to hear on any subject—yet somehow he makes the whole procedure curiously fascinating."

Maybe oranges and bark canoes aren't such boring topics after all.

Writer Tracy Kidder has also tackled some non-sexy subjects—from building a computer in *The Soul of a New Machine* to building a *House*. "You can write about *anything*," says Kidder, "and if you write well enough, even the reader with no intrinsic interest in the subject will become involved."

"BUT RESEARCH IS SO BORING."

Depends how you do your research. Hemingway went deep-sea fishing (*The Old Man and the Sea*), Steinbeck lived with migrant workers (*The Grapes of Wrath*) and Truman Capote talked with a couple of killers (*In Cold Blood*). More recently, Peter Mayle did his research while living the good life in the south of France. The result was a best-seller, *A Year in Provence*, followed by *another* best-seller, *Toujours Provence*.

But research is boring?

No more than sipping Bordeaux, munching on fresh Camembert and getting *paid* to write about it.

When Waldo Salt did his research for the screenplay for *Coming Home*, transcripts of his interviews with Vietnam paraplegics totaled 1,500 pages. Maybe that's why *Coming Home* won an Oscar for Best Screenplay.

POP QUIZ # 3

(Another ten questions you can't get wrong)

1. Stop rejecting your thoughts and start _____.
   a) cleaning house
   b) going for long, moody walks
   c) a day-care center for frustrated writers
   d) writing them down

2. What's needed is entitlement—the firm belief that "If it interests me, it will _____ others."
   a) annoy
   b) torment
   c) nauseate
   d) interest

3. Likewise, if it matters to you, it will _____.
   a) keep you awake at night
   b) put your readers to sleep
   c) never be on sale
   d) matter to others

4. As George Bernard Shaw observed: "The man who writes about himself and his own time is the only man who writes about _____."
   a) ten minutes a day
   b) setting his alarm clock
   c) boring, meaningless, self-indulgent crap
   d) all people and all time

5. If Ben Hamper can write about riveting and Mary Cahill can write about carpooling, then you can write about _____.
   a) riveting
   b) carpooling
   c) flossing your feet
   d) anything you want

6. Whatever you do, do not stick to: "Just the _____, ma'am."
   a) Spam
   b) ham
   c) green eggs and ham
   d) facts

7. Hold a mirror up to your life. But make it a _____ mirror.
   a) clean
   b) dirty
   c) self-cleaning
   d) fun-house

8. Think of your writing as a letter to the editor. The world according to _____.
   a) Garp
   b) Sartre
   c) Leonard Nimoy
   d) You

9. As Robert Frost said: "No tears in the writer, no _____."
   a) fish in the water
   b) dishes in the sink
   c) beers for nobody
   d) tears in the reader

10. William Goldman says that it took him eight years to write *Butch Cassidy and the Sundance Kid* because _____.
   a) he can only type with his nose
   b) his dog ate his typewriter
   c) he was being paid by the hour
   d) he did a lot of research

Answer Key: 1) d, 2) d, 3) d, 4) d, 5) d, 6) d, 7) d, 8) d, 9) d, 10) d

Part Four

Writing
vs.
Rewriting

——————— OR ———————
*OKAY, I'VE FINALLY GOT
A FIRST DRAFT.
NOW WHAT?*

20

HOW COULD YOU SAY SOMETHING SO STUPID?

A woman I was dating once yelled at me: "You're a writer, how could you say something so stupid?"

"That's why I'm a writer. I get to rewrite myself."

When we talk, we're all over the place—going this way, that way, backtracking, making a detour, losing our train of thought, finding it, losing it again—an endless series of "fits and starts." Figuring it out as we go, we give a sloppy, meandering—and, yes, sometimes stupid-sounding—presentation.

Spoken language is *incredibly* imprecise. If you've ever seen a word-for-word transcript, you know what I mean. Filled with half sentences and disjointed thoughts, they're almost impossible to follow:

That's why, you know, if you take everything into account and all, because— Well, if you don't, you miss the shipping date and everyone sort of suffers, because it's not the same as what they expected and— Anyway, then there's no room for—you know, the next guy to make it up. So everyone tries their best to at least—you know—do what they can and make sure there's no confusion left.

No confusion left? No wonder there are so many misunderstandings when we talk.

Think of talking, or "talking" on paper, as trying to drive somewhere without directions. All that matters is that you eventually get from point A to point B, no matter how long or circuitous a route you take or how many times you nearly get lost. The real test is to see what happens when you turn around and head back. Aware of the "wrong turns," or detours, you made in getting there, you can now make your journey home a lot simpler and less confusing. Or at least that's the goal.

Likewise, having gone "Blah, blah, blah" to produce your first draft, you now have the opportunity to go back and *revise* your words—to make them simpler and less confusing, and to look a lot smarter on paper than you might sound in person.

Remember: Writing is a two-step process. First you find the gold, then you go back and polish it.

❏

This is what I find most encouraging about the writing trades:
They allow mediocre people who are patient and
industrious to revise their stupidity, to edit themselves into
something like intelligence. They also allow lunatics
to seem saner than sane.

—Kurt Vonnegut

❏

WARNING

If you're finally writing after being blocked or bunched up for years, don't even *think* about rewriting. For now, learn to enjoy the freedom and spontaneity of simply "talking" on paper. You might stay at this stage for weeks, even months. Move on to rewriting when you're *ready* to move on—not just because it's the next chapter.

"But I'm only halfway through the book."

You're halfway to being cured. Skip this section and move on to Part Five: Rules of the Road. (Better yet, keep writing and don't even worry about the rest of the book.)

❑

Sitting in a coffee shop, I watched a young woman scribble away into a notebook, writing as fast as her hand could manage. She kept up the pace for twenty minutes or so, then put down her pen and closed the notebook with a look of accomplishment.

"What are you working on?" I asked.

"I don't know, I'm just writing."

As it turned out, Arianna wrote nearly every day. Sometimes at the coffee shop, sometimes at home. She'd been writing like this for years—bits of stories, random notes, anything that crossed her mind.

"Don't you ever go back and look things over? Try to shape them into something?"

"Look back? I'm too busy going ahead!"

Let Arianna be your role model: If you discover that throwing words on paper is so exciting you can't do anything but turn the page and keep writing, *turn the page and keep writing!* Write on. Don't look back. Fill as many notebooks as you like and forget about rewriting. That's step one: enjoying yourself.

Step two begins when you decide to up the ante—when it's time to turn *this* page and start rewriting.

21

FIRST, WAIT AWHILE

Now that you've got something down on paper, you'll have the heady experience of someone who *has* written, an experience that will either be terrific, terrifying or both.

This is a time for major celebration. *You put your fears aside and wrote something.* Reward yourself by taking a break and getting some distance on what you've done. Go for a walk, have a beer, take in a movie or do all three.

Coming back to your work, you'll discover that it's not as great or terrible as you'd imagined; the truth will always lie somewhere in the middle. What you needed was objectivity—the ability to read what you've written as if you were the *reader*, not the writer.

How long will that take?

The longer you stay away, the more objectivity you'll gain—though try not to wait so long that your boss calls you up screaming, "I don't care what Saltzman says, we need it now!"

As a rule, waiting just an hour or two can make a major difference in your ability to see things more clearly. Even better is waiting overnight, returning to your work in the clear light of day. For the real acid test, try waiting a few months. *Guaranteed*: You'll be so objective you'll be able to read the work as if it were, well, someone else's. You'll see what works, what doesn't and just how much work that other person has in front of him.

❏

The feeling that the work is magnificent, and the feeling that it is abominable, are both mosquitoes to be repelled, ignored, or killed, but not indulged.

—Annie Dillard

Truly, I've seldom seen a piece of prose, or a poem—my own or anyone else's—that couldn't be improved upon if it were left alone for a time.

—Raymond Carver

❏

Having finished his first draft of *A Farewell to Arms*, Ernest Hemingway wrote in a letter to his editor, Max Perkins: "Would like to put it away for a couple or three months and then re-write it. The re-writing doesn't take more than six weeks or two months once it is done. But it is pretty important for me to let it cool off well before re-writing."

Then, in a follow-up: "I want to make sure I leave it alone long enough so I can find the places where I get the kick when writing it and neglect to convey it to the reader."

22

READ IT OUT LOUD

Time to cross your fingers, take a deep breath . . . and read it out loud. This forces you to hear your words the way your reader will. You'll hear what sounds like talking and what sounds like "writing."

Reading it out loud, you will *never* be able to keep a sentence that reads: *Good attendance to include being at work on time is expected as well as a condition of employment.* If you do find such a sentence, cross it out; then ask yourself, "What am I trying to say here?" and *say* it by "talking" on paper.

WANT TO GET DARING?

Try reading your work to someone else. See where their eyes glaze over, or where they light up.

Remember the homework assignment I give to my students, "Write two paragraphs as badly as possible"? Next class, they read them out loud. No exceptions. Everyone reads.

What happens is that no matter how dreadful someone thinks their work is, the class usually hears it as "not so bad" after all. Sometimes, they even "like" what they've heard. So don't be so quick to condemn your work as garbage. (Or yourself, for that matter.) Reading out loud, try to listen to your words with fresh, open ears. Ask yourself: "If someone else wrote this, objectively, what would I think?" That's your goal—to listen to your work as if it were written by someone else.

Steinbeck, in fact, would write in longhand, then read into a tape recorder. "[Y]ou can hear the most terrible things you've done if you hear it clear back on tape," he explained. "I do it particularly with dialogue because then I can find whether it sounds like speech or not."

Again, you might also hear what sounds pretty good. As Steinbeck himself admitted in a 1938 journal entry: "I read a couple of chapters [of *The Grapes of Wrath*] to friends last night and could see the whole thing clearly. Also it doesn't sound bad."

WANT TO GET REALLY DARING?

Take what you've written and have someone read it to you. See how *you* like the sound of it.

Years ago, back in New York, I signed up for a course in playwriting. Still in my "angry young man" phase, everything I wrote was dark, brooding and hopping mad. Making me even madder was the teacher's mandate that we would not be reading our own material. Instead, we were to hand out copies of our scenes, assigning the different roles to various students who'd no doubt mangle and misinterpret everything I'd written.

The first time the class read my work not only did they "misinterpret" it, they laughed at it. No because it was bad, mind you, but because the class thought it funny. (This is the worst thing you can do to an "angry young man"—laugh at his misery.) Determined to get the upper hand, I went home and wrote a scene that was *really* angry. Problem was they laughed again; only this time the laughs were bigger.

After six or seven weeks of torturous laughter, it suddenly occurred to me: *Maybe I should be writing comedy instead.*

WHATEVER YOU DO, DON'T APOLOGIZE

When reading your work out loud—even if you're the only person in the room—never read in a weak, apologetic mumble. Read in a strong, "this is important" voice. Reading with apology means reading to your inner critic; reading with conviction means finding your own voice.

23

BUT IT'S NOT EVEN CLOSE TO PERFECT

Having just read your first draft, you must now avoid the pitfall of beating yourself up because it "should" be perfect and it's not even close. Instead, learn to say to yourself: "Parts of this are not as good as they could be; but it *will* get better as I start to rewrite it." Again:

PROGRESS, NOT PERFECTION

Meanwhile, if you're feeling overwhelmed by all the work it's going to take to "get it in shape," rest assured this is a typical reaction. It's the same way you felt about the blank page at first—overwhelmed by it all. You got over that fear, you'll get over this one.

For now, keep in mind that when a particular piece of writing *looks* nice and easy, chances are it took a lot of hard work to make it look that easy. In other words:

DON'T BE DECEIVED BY SOMEONE ELSE'S POLISHED DRAFT

Writing takes work. A lot of work. It's a slow, meticulous, painstaking task—sometimes rewarding, sometimes so maddening, writes Joan Didion, "that there is always a point in the writing of a piece when I sit in a room literally papered with false starts and cannot put one word after another and imagine that I have suffered a small stroke, leaving me apparently undamaged but actually aphasic." (And you thought *you* had it rough?)

Stick with it long enough, though, and chaos turns to order: Each problem reveals a solution, rough edges are smoothed just so and the thing starts to fly the way it was meant to fly. That's when you step back from the finished product and feel like screaming: *It's so obvious. What the hell took me so long?*

The answer is simple. Like any puzzle, it's always easy *after* you've solved it. "I have worked for years," said Henri Matisse, "in order that people might say, 'It seems so easy to do.'"

It does seem easy—if you let yourself be deceived by someone else's polished draft, that is.

□

A clear sentence is no accident. Very few sentences come out right the first time, or even the third time. Remember this as a consolation in moments of despair.
      —William Zinsser

I begin a painting with a series of mistakes. The painting comes out of the correction of mistakes by feeling.
      —Robert Motherwell

□

HOW TO MAKE A TERRIFIC SALAD DRESSING

Mix up some olive oil, Dijon mustard and balsamic vinegar. Now take a taste and ask yourself: "Do I need more olive oil? More vinegar? Maybe I need *less* vinegar." This is the only way I know to make a terrific salad dressing: Mix up a batch. Taste it. Mix again.

The "secret ingredient" is the patience to keep trying—to keep working at it till you get it just right.

Do most people have the talent to make a terrific salad dressing? *Absolutely.*

Are they willing to make the effort to develop that skill? *That's a different question.*

24

WHAT AM I TRYING TO SAY, ANYWAY?

After writing your first draft, you let it "cool off well." Then you read it out loud and realized it wasn't even close to perfect. Now take three giant steps backward and ask yourself: "What am I trying to say, anyway?"

As painter Jackson Pollock wrote:

When I am *in* my painting, I am not aware of what I'm doing.[1] It is only after a sort of "get acquainted" period that I see what I have been about. I have no fears about making changes, destroying the image, etc., because the painting has a life of its own. I try to let it come through. It is only when I lose contact with the painting that the result is a mess. Otherwise there is pure harmony, an easy give and take, and the painting comes out well.

Don't worry, it's not as "mystical" as it sounds.

Think of your first draft as a map to buried treasure: All the markers are there, but you've still got a way to go. Maybe it's buried deep below the surface and it's going to take some digging before you unearth it; or maybe it's right in front of you and all you have to do is open your eyes.

[1]You might call this his *freepainting* phase, throwing paint and ideas down on canvas.

You'll find your answer by following the various clues presented in your first draft, in mulling over each phrase or idea and asking yourself: "Is this what I'm trying to say? What about this idea over here?"

"Maybe I revise," wrote Raymond Carver, "because it gradually takes me into the heart of what the story is *about*. I have to keep trying to see if I can find that out. It's a process more than a fixed position.

"There was a time when I used to think it was a character defect that made me have to struggle along like this. I don't think this way any longer."

Forget the idea that you're still a beginner or have some "character defect" that makes finding your meaning tougher than you *think* it should be. Finding your meaning is never easy. That's why people are always saying to one another: "What do you *mean* exactly?" (Or why I've been struggling to rewrite this paragraph for the past hour or so.) Because finding your meaning and expressing it clearly is no easy task.

Remember: If you don't know what you're trying to say at first, that's okay; and if you have to "struggle along" for a while, that's okay, too. It's more than okay; it's the only way you'll get to say: "Now I know what I've been trying to say all this time!"

❑

. . . [It's] a kind of whittling, a honing to the bone, until
you finally get whatever the hell it is you're looking
for. It's an exercise in sculpture, chipping away at the rock
until you find the nose.

—Stanley Elkin

❑

There's an old joke about a private in the army who spends his spare time wandering around, searching for scraps of paper. Each time he finds a scrap he picks it up, looks it over and says: "That's not it." He goes on like this week after week. "That's not it. That's not it." Finally, they give him a psychiatric examination and hand him his discharge. He looks it over, stands up and says: "That's it!"

This is what happens when you go through your first draft, asking yourself: "Is this what I'm trying to say? What about this idea over here?" It's going to take some searching, all right. But when you find the answer, there'll be no doubt about it.

25

WHEN IN DOUBT, THROW OUT

Now that you know what you're trying to say (or at least have a sense of it), it's time to get rid of everything that doesn't help you say it.

Imagine you're weeding out your closet, looking over each piece of clothing and posing hard-nosed questions: "Do I really need this shirt with a stain on the pocket? What about those bell-bottoms from the sixties? And how many raggedy T-shirts can I sleep in anyway?"

True, these are pretty simple questions. But when they're *your* clothes, *your* words, it's not so simple to let them go. *Let them go; let a lot of them go.*

"Be merciless on yourself," writes Kurt Vonnegut. "If a sentence does not illuminate your subject in some new and useful way, scratch it out."

TRUE CONFESSION

Two paragraphs above, there's a sentence that reads: "Let them go; let a lot of them go." In an earlier draft—in a *number* of earlier drafts—the thought continued: "Besides, they're not even your words; you only borrowed them."

I really liked those lines; I fell in love with them. I liked their sound, their humor, even their preachiness. But then I got tough with myself, asked myself the kinds of questions I was telling you to ask. "Okay," I said, "they *sound* nice, but do I really need them? Could I honestly walk up to Kurt Vonnegut and say, 'Yes, they illuminate my subject in a new and useful way'?"

So out they went. I let them go. I let ten precious, scintillating words evaporate from the page, never to be seen or heard from again.[1] I was merciless. When you're looking to cut, it's the only way to be.

❑

Creation really begins for me when I have a first version of the novel, when I have to choose, to select, to eliminate everything that is not worthwhile for the development of the story.

—*Mario Vargas Llosa*

❑

The most essential gift for a good writer is a built-in, shock-proof shit detector.

—*Ernest Hemingway*

❑

I always listen for what I can leave out.

—*Miles Davis*

---

[1] Then again, I did find a way to use my ten words—even if it was to show you why I had to get rid of them. "In my case," said Picasso, "a picture is a sum of destructions. I do a picture—then I destroy it. In the end, though, nothing is lost; the red I took away from one place turns up somewhere else."

THUMBS DOWN, THUMBS UP

In 1991, Gene Siskel and Roger Ebert reviewed a movie called *A Rage in Harlem* and both gave it "Thumbs Down." A few weeks later, they viewed another cut of the film—pared from 120 to 110 minutes. (It was this version that was released to local theaters.) With just 10 minutes cut from the film, Siskel and Ebert *both* changed their vote from "Thumbs Down" to "Thumbs Up."

Even so, added Siskel: "I still think it's too long."

Reading Exercise:
"Let's Find Saltzman"

To help you appreciate how throwing things out can improve your work, I've "collaborated" with a number of first-rate authors by taking samples of their work and adding unnecessary words and phrases. Your job is to read over these bloated samples, "find Saltzman" and cross out the junk. You'll be left with the original gems—outstanding samples we'd all be proud to call our own.

INSTRUCTIONS

Read the first sample (Bastardized Version) out loud and ask yourself what the author is trying to say—the same thing you'd do with your own first draft. Then take a pencil and put a line through everything that's fatty or extra—everything that does *not* help the story. When you're done see how your version compares to the original (Published Version). Reading the Published Version out loud, hear how much stronger and self-assured it sounds *without* all the fat.

Then move on to the following samples, trying to make them as lean as possible.

WARNING

This is not a test, it's an *exercise*. Do not grade yourself on how well your editing choices match with the original. Just try to learn from the process and see how much better things read without all the fat.

SAMPLE ONE:
BASTARDIZED VERSION

Consider the opening paragraphs of Raymond Carver's short story "Elephant" as expanded and *not* improved by yours truly:

I knew it was a mistake to let my lousy, irresponsible brother have the money. I didn't need anybody else owing me, that's for sure. But when he called on that rainy night and said he couldn't make the payment on his house, what could I do? I'd never been inside his house—he lived a thousand miles away, in California—I'd never even *seen* his split-level, Craftsman–style house—but I didn't want him to lose it. He cried over the phone and said he was losing everything he worked for. He said he'd pay me back. He swore to me. February, he said. Maybe sooner. No later, anyway, than March. April, tops. He said his income tax refund was on the way. Plus, he said, he had a little investment that would mature in February. Then he snorted a little laugh, thinking how he wasn't too mature, himself. But his investment *would* mature, even if he hadn't. He acted secretive about the investment thing, so I didn't press for details.

"Trust me on this," he said. "I know I've lied to you before. I know I haven't been the greatest brother you could ask for. I know all that. But this time, cross my heart, I won't let you down."

SAMPLE ONE:
PUBLISHED VERSION

I knew it was a mistake to let my ~~lousy, irresponsible~~ brother have the money. I didn't need anybody else owing me~~, that's for sure~~. But when he called ~~on that rainy night~~ and said he couldn't make the payment on his house, what could I do? I'd never been inside his house—he lived a thousand miles away, in California—I'd never even *seen* his ~~split-level, Craftsman-style~~ house—but I didn't want him to lose it. He cried over the phone and said he was losing everything he worked for. He said he'd pay me back. ~~He swore to me.~~ February, he said. Maybe sooner. No later, anyway, than March. ~~April, tops.~~ He said his income tax refund was on the way. Plus, he said, he had a little investment that would mature in February. ~~Then he snorted a little laugh, thinking how he wasn't too mature, himself. But his investment *would* mature, even if he hadn't.~~ He acted secretive about the investment thing, so I didn't press for details.

"Trust me on this," he said. ~~"I know I've lied to you before. I know I haven't been the greatest brother you could ask for. I know all that. But this time, cross my heart,~~ I won't let you down."

—from "Elephant," by Raymond Carver

SAMPLE TWO:
BASTARDIZED VERSION

From the essay "Have a Good Day," in *I Must Say,* by Edwin Newman. Extra words and phrases by Joel Saltzman:

Good old "Have a good day." There is no way of getting around it. Not on the check-out line, not on the bus, not in the elevator. Everybody in sight or hearing is forever wishing you one, including people you don't know, will never see again, *pray* you never see again, and who don't care whether you have a good day or step into a deep puddle and ruin your shoes, break a leg at the next intersection, or even worse. So pervasive is this that even New York City buses, in big, bright signs above the windshield, join in the never-ending chorus. It would not be surprising to hear that Indian tribes from out West somewhere send up smoke signals wishing one another a good day, and that muggers wearing ski masks, making off with their loot, say it obnoxiously to their victims.

SAMPLE TWO:
PUBLISHED VERSION

Good old "Have a good day." There is no way of getting around it. ~~Not on the check-out line, not on the bus, not in the elevator.~~ Everybody in sight or hearing is forever wishing you one, including people you don't know, will never see again, ~~pray you never see again,~~ and who don't care whether you have a good day or ~~step into a deep puddle and ruin your shoes,~~ break a leg at the next intersection~~, or even worse~~. So pervasive is this that even New York City buses, in ~~big, bright~~ signs above the windshield, join in the ~~never-ending~~ chorus. It would not be surprising to hear that Indian tribes ~~from out West somewhere~~ send up smoke signals wishing one another a good day, and that muggers ~~wearing ski masks~~, making off with their loot, say it ~~obnoxiously~~ to their victims.

— from "Have a Good Day," by Edwin Newman

SAMPLE THREE:
BASTARDIZED VERSION

From *A Yellow Raft in Blue Water*, by Michael Dorris, muddied up by Joel Saltzman:

I'm not that hard for Evelyn to find. If she wanted to, she could find me easily. I'm stopped, halfway down the steep, rugged trail, with my eyes fixed on the empty yellow raft floating in the blue waters of Bearpaw Lake. Somewhere in my mind, I don't know where exactly, I've decided that if I stare at it long and hard enough it will launch me out of my present troubles. If I squint at it a certain way, in fact, it appears to be a lighted trapdoor, flush against a black floor. With my eyes closed almost completely, it becomes a kind of bull's-eye, and I'm an arrow, sharp and ready, totally determined, banging into it head-first.

SAMPLE THREE:
PUBLISHED VERSION

I'm not that hard for Evelyn to find. ~~If she wanted to, she could find me easily.~~ I'm stopped, halfway down the ~~steep, rugged~~ trail, with my eyes fixed on the empty yellow raft floating in the blue waters of Bearpaw Lake. Somewhere in my mind~~, I don't know where exactly,~~ I decided that if I stare at it ~~long and~~ hard enough it will launch me out of my present troubles. If I squint at it a certain way, ~~in fact,~~ it appears to be a lighted trapdoor, flush against a black floor. With my eyes closed almost completely, it becomes a kind of bull's-eye, and I'm an arrow~~, sharp and ready, totally determined,~~ banging into it head-first.

  —from *A Yellow Raft in Blue Water*, by Michael Dorris

SAMPLE FOUR:
BASTARDIZED VERSION

From *Geek Love*, by Katherine Dunn, made less lovely by Joel Saltzman:

It was a story about a very young boy, fourteen, maybe fifteen or so, and Peggy claimed it was one-hundred percent true. He died for love, she said, simple as that. His family was dirt poor. He was cut out for heavy, laborious work and bad pay, but he was a sweet kid, and he loved a blond, blue-eyed cheerleader in his school. She wouldn't even look at him, of course, no big surprise there. Her life was different— like someone from another planet. But then she got really sick and the doctors said it was her heart. She would die, they said, unless she could get a new one and then they could do a transplant. The word went around the school that she was doing nothing but waiting for a donor. The boy was terribly sad for a while, but then he got a great idea and told his mother that he was going to die and give his heart to the girl. His mother thought this was just his dumbness and sweetness talking. He was healthy as an ox. But a few days later he dropped dead. Instantly. Right there in the middle of the bathroom one morning while his mother was downstairs frying the bacon. A brain hemorrhage, they said. Surprisingly, the doctors found that his bits actually were compatible to the cheerleader's bits, and they transplanted his fresh heart right into her. It worked. Now she dances and cheers and even goes roller-skating with the poor boy's heart.

SAMPLE FOUR:
PUBLISHED VERSION

It was ~~a story~~ about a very young boy, fourteen~~, maybe fifteen~~ or so, and Peggy claimed it was ~~one-hundred per-cent~~ true. He died for love, she said~~, simple as that~~. His family was dirt poor. He was cut out for heavy~~, laborious~~ work and bad pay, but he was a sweet kid, and he loved a ~~blond, blue-eyed~~ cheerleader in his school. She wouldn't even look at him, of course~~, no big surprise there~~. Her life was different—~~like someone from another planet~~. But then she got ~~really~~ sick and the doctors said it was her heart. She would die, they said, unless she could get a new one ~~and then they could do a transplant~~. The word went around the school that she was ~~doing nothing but~~ waiting for a donor. The boy was terribly sad for a while, but then he ~~got a great idea and~~ told his mother that he was going to die and give his heart to the girl. His mother thought this was just his ~~dumbness and~~ sweetness talking. He was healthy ~~as an ox~~. But a few days later he dropped dead. Instantly. ~~Right there in the middle of the bathroom one morning while his mother was downstairs frying the bacon.~~ A brain hemorrhage, they said. Surprisingly, the doctors found that his bits actually were compatible to the cheerleader's ~~bits~~, and they transplanted his fresh heart right into her. It worked. Now she dances and cheers ~~and even goes roller-skating~~ with the poor boy's heart.

—from *Geek Love*, by Katherine Dunn

WHAT HAPPENS IF YOU DON'T CUT THE FAT?

People don't like it.

There's an old writer's adage: "If I had more time, I would have written less." Give yourself the extra time. Write less and say it better.

□

I find I have . . . a tendency to overwrite, to use two or three words where one will do it better. I have to go back and cut and cut.

—*John Steinbeck*

□

26

TINKER, TAILOR, TINKER SOME MORE

Remember those comic books where the headline would read: "What's wrong in this picture?" You'd study every inch of it, examining even the smallest details, asking yourself: "Is this right? What about that man wearing one shoe? And let's count the legs on that dog, looks like he might have a few extra."

Study your first draft in much the same way. Look it over line by line. Ask yourself: "Is this right? What about this sentence? Should I change it; leave it; put it somewhere else? Maybe I should dump it altogether."

Think of yourself as the building inspector—making a thorough examination of the work in progress and refusing to "sign off" till you know it's structurally sound.

"But it's got so many problems, I don't know what to do."

Play with it.

In *Self-Renewal*, education innovator John W. Gardner (not to be confused with the novelist John Gardner) describes a creative person as someone who "will toy with an idea, 'try it on for size,' look at it from a dozen different angles.... Unlike the rest of us, they do not persist stubbornly in one approach to a problem. They can change directions and shift energies.

They can give up their initial perception of a problem and redefine it."

This is the best definition I know for the process of rewriting—being "creative" enough to examine your work without being bound by your *first* way of doing things.

"But how do I know if I'm going in the right direction, if I'm making it better and not worse?"

You don't.

"I see all the faults," Amy Tan told the *New York Times*. "I know what's been put in and what's been taken out. I know where the mistakes are, and I'm always afraid someone's going to catch them and say, 'You put the wrong emphasis on this,' or 'You used the wrong angle on that.'"

There are very few absolutes when it comes to rewriting. All you can do is take your best shot and hope for the best, hope you didn't zig where you should have zagged.

Remember: Study the page, play with it, "look at it from a dozen different angles." Try it one way, then another, then another again, all the time keeping in mind: "This is a game, not brain surgery."

❑

*I like to mess around with my stories. I'd rather tinker with
a story after writing it, and then tinker some more,
changing this, changing that, than have to write the story
in the first place. That initial writing just seems to me
the hard place I have to get to in order to go on and have
fun with the story.*

—Raymond Carver

*A lot depends on having the right spirit: businesslike and
detached. A certain ruthlessness is best of all. Not
desperate-ruthlessness, "Oh, God, this is* awful, *I've got
to change* everything," *but breezy-ruthlessness, "Yes,
this certainly does have some problems."*

—Peter Elbow

❑

THE ELEGANT SOLUTION

Part of the game involves searching for what scientists call an elegant solution.

When my cousin Elliot and I were kids we were playing miniature golf and lost one of the balls. Heading back to the equipment desk, worrying what our punishment would be, we spotted a large sign that read: ALL CLUBS MUST BE RETURNED WITH A BALL. Suddenly, we discovered an elegant solution: *We threw one of the clubs away.* And that was that.

27

MAKE IT AS SIMPLE AS POSSIBLE

Another part of the game is learning to simplify. For example, this chapter used to be called: "Try to Make It as Simple as Possible." Now it's simpler—and better.

Ever compliment someone on an outfit they're wearing and they shoot back with: "This? It's just something I threw together at the last minute"? *Baloney*. Casual clothing may *look* real casual but it takes a lot of effort to look that effortless.

SHOPPING FOR SIMPLICITY

I used to live in a neighborhood where there were a lot of clothing boutiques. Taking a break from writing, now and then, I'd wander over and check out the stores. At one store—known for its avant-garde fashions—I'd look at the clothing and shrug: "I don't get it." Then I'd walk a few stores down to the Gap and everything I looked at made sense. Here was clothing that was so *simple* and easy to understand you didn't need a fine arts degree to appreciate it.

Once in a while, though, I would see something that didn't quite make sense. Then I'd look a little closer and invariably I'd see an "On Sale" sign. *Now* it made sense.

Here was an article of clothing where the designer failed to work hard enough to make it so simple that anyone could take one look at it and say: "Oh, I get it."

Same goes for writing: If it looks nice and easy, chances are it took a lot of hard work; but if it looks wordy and complicated, chances are it was very easy to write. Easy to write, maybe, but how much fun is it to read something that's a lot more complicated than it needs to be?

FOR EXAMPLE

My first draft of this section included the line: "I used to live near Melrose Avenue, in Los Angeles, where a string of clothing boutiques range from European-trendy to American-casual." Not a *bad* sentence, but how much of it was really necessary for the story? Going over it a few times, I *simplified* it until it read: "I used to live in a neighborhood where there were a lot of clothing boutiques."

Simple. Direct. Right to the point.

Imagine you're a bounty hunter looking for work. One thing you could do is send out a long letter introducing yourself, stating your unique qualifications and assuring your prospective employer of your "willingness to relocate." Or, like Richard Boone on the old TV show, you could hand out a card that simply read: "Have Gun, Will Travel."

"But as a writer, can you really make it that simple?"

Why not?

Ellen Gilchrist, in her short story "The Young Man," starts out: "This is a story about an old lady who ordered a man from an L. L. Bean catalog."

Can't get much simpler than that.

Or consider Tobias Wolff, whose story "The Rich Brother" begins: "There were two brothers, Pete and Donald.

"Pete, the older brother, was in real estate. He and his wife had a Century 21 franchise in Santa Cruz. Pete worked hard and made a lot of money, but not any more than he thought he deserved. He had two daughters, a sailboat, a house from which he could see a thin slice of the ocean, and friends doing well enough in their own lives not to wish bad luck on him. Donald, the younger brother, was still single. He lived alone, painted houses when he found the work, and got deeper in debt to Pete when he didn't."

Simple. Direct. Right to the point.

How do you get that simple?

You work at it.

□

It is only through hard work that I can give an impression of ease and simplicity. I must strive to erase all traces of effort and to reach clarity and purity.

—Henri Matisse

□

The key word here is "impression"—an *impression* of ease and simplicity. To give that impression, you must first work hard and then "erase all traces of effort." This is why you must never compare your half-baked, struggling-for-definition work to the "clarity and purity" of the masters. Doing so, you neglect a basic fact of creative evolution: The professional works as hard as possible to make it look as easy as possible. *The finished product is a huge sleight of hand.*

Consider the "effortless" dancing of Fred Astaire and Ginger Rogers—hard, diligent work that gave the *impression* of ease and simplicity. Or think about a typical dinner party. The guests arrive and everything's laid out nice and neat. But what was it like just half an hour ago? *Pandemonium*, that's what.

A friend of mine met Julia Child at a cocktail party and asked her how she managed to keep her kitchen so tidy when she cooked. "My dear, you have no idea. It's a *disaster* when I'm finished!"

"But it always looks so perfect."

"That's because I've been throwing everything on the floor. You just don't see it on television!"

Remember: Hide your tracks. Bury each tortured effort. Show the reader nothing but your smooth, final copy—deceive us with your *own* polished prose.

☐

A writer's best friend is the wastepaper basket.
                                        —Isaac Bashevis Singer

☐

EFFORTLESS SINGING

Describing the singing of opera soprano Barbara Hendricks, Dennis McFarland wrote in the New York Times: "There's no grimacing, no visible evidence of breath-control or sound-production, and you have the feeling that Ms. Hendricks is singing with the voice she was born with, not with one she made for herself.... This is not to suggest that she hasn't had to work hard, like all musicians of merit—but she has had the good sense not to train her voice into something that *sounds* trained."

Like Matisse, Hendricks has strived to "erase all traces of effort." The result *appears* to be effortless, but we certainly know better.

EFFORTLESS WRITING

Reviewing the 1991 film *Toto le Héro (Toto the Hero)*, Vincent Canby wrote in the New York Times: "*Toto* has the self-assurance and the gusto of something that might have been conceived in a single spasm of creativity. It flies effortlessly from one time period to another, from one mood to its opposite. It seems never to have been fiddled with, rewritten or sweated over."

What's the punch line?
The screenplay for *Toto* took five years to write.

28

DON'T BE AFRAID
TO ADD OR EXPAND

Rewriting can also mean adding, or making it longer.

For my first draft, the line you just read was the sum total of this chapter. That's all I could think of, and I knew I'd have to go back and say more later. Having "slept" on it for a while, I was able to add:

In an essay about growing up, a student writes: "Why was Daddy getting drunk that night? Was mother having fun or just pretending? Was brother Jack around, or off sneaking a smoke somewhere? And where was I, a little three-year-old?"
Clearly, a passage like this could lead to a strong story all by itself. Yet this is where the writer pulls the plug and abruptly ends her piece, leaving the reader—and herself—with more questions than answers.

**IF YOU ARE PROVOKED TO ASK GOOD QUESTIONS,
PROVOKE YOURSELF TO GO BACK AND ANSWER THEM.**

"But what if I don't *have* any questions?"
Dig a little deeper.

Ask yourself the kinds of questions a good reporter would ask: Who? What? When? Where? Why? How? How much? Can I get a discount if I pay cash?

Imagine you're shopping for a new stereo. You wouldn't ask the salesman one or two questions, you'd ask *dozens* of questions. When you're writing, you're the salesman—trying to convince the reader of X or Y, or at least getting them to see X or Y the way *you* want them to see it. That's your job: answering questions, anticipating them, assuring the reader that your position is solid, well thought out and one worth buying.

Writing your first draft, don't expect to find all the answers. And don't stop because you're stuck on some point or need to research a fact. You're much better off putting a *blank* here and there, or writing a note to yourself: "To be expanded." When Joan Didion was writing her first draft of *Play It As It Lays*, she'd mark places "chapter to come." Then she went back and filled in the blanks.

For your first draft, write what you can, then move on. Don't worry that it's "skimpy" or "not enough." You can always go back and make it better. *You better go back and make it better.*

"What are you going to do, beat me up?"

No, but your readers might.

❑

Push it. Examine all things intensely and relentlessly.
                                        —*Annie Dillard*

Rewriting Exercises: "Tell Us More"

Read through one of your first drafts and find a line, or paragraph, where the reader might want to know more. Ask yourself: "If I were talking and told you only this much, would you want to know more?"

Now go back and use *guided freewriting* to tell us more. A lot more. Tell us everything you know and then some.

I remember the day I finished *Ironweed*. I came down and I said, "I'm finished." My wife was there and one of my good friends; they had read most of the book along the way and they sat down and read the ending. Somehow they didn't respond the way I wanted them to respond. I was thinking of an abstract reader who would say what every writer wants you to say to him: "This is the best thing I ever read in my life." I knew something was wrong, though I didn't know what; I knew the elements of the ending should be very powerful. I thought about it and their lack of proper response. After dinner I went back upstairs and rewrote the ending, adding a page and a half. I brought that down and then they said, "This is the best thing I've ever read in my life."

—William Kennedy, from *Writers at Work: The Paris Review Interviews*

POP QUIZ #4

(Ten more questions you can't get wrong)

1. Writing is a two-step process. First you find the gold, then you _____
   a) sell it
   b) hide it
   c) become rich and famous
   d) polish it

2. What you need is objectivity—the ability to read what you've written as if you were the _____, not the writer.
   a) Duke of Earl
   b) Dukes of Hazzard
   c) Pulitzer Prize Evaluation Committee
   d) reader

3. Reading your work out loud, you'll hear what sounds like talking and what sounds like _____.
   a) barking
   b) singing
   c) whistling
   d) "writing"

4. After reading your first draft, learn to say to yourself: "Parts of this are not as good as they could be; but it *will* get better as I _____."
   a) season to taste
   b) throw it out and start over
   c) hire a *real* writer
   d) start to rewrite it

5. When in doubt, _____.
   a) see a shrink
   b) see a movie

   c) throw up
   d) throw out

6. If I had more time, I would have written _____.
   a) more
   b) a lot more
   c) something worth reading
   d) less

7. When you're rewriting, make it as simple as _____.
   a) nuclear fission
   b) DNA
   c) Einstein's theory of relativity
   d) possible

8. If the final product *looks* nice and easy, chances are it took a lot of _____.
   a) tinkering
   b) tailoring
   c) time and patience
   d) all of the above

9. According to Isaac Bashevis Singer: "A writer's best friend is the _____."
   a) Scotch
   b) Vodka
   c) white wine spritzer
   d) wastepaper basket

10. Writing your first draft, don't worry that it's "skimpy" or "not enough." You can always go back and make it _____.
   a) fatter
   b) plumper
   c) juicier
   d) better

Answer Key: 1) d, 2) d, 3) d, 4) d, 5) d, 6) d, 7) d, 8) d, 9) d, 10) d

Part Five

Rules

of the

Road

29

PROGRESS,
NOT PERFECTION

Whether you're struggling with a single sentence or polishing a book-length manuscript, let progress be your guide, not perfection your nemesis. Apply this life-preserving rule of thumb not just to your current work, but to your *body* of work.

"Every time you go into a project you convince yourself it's great," says television writer and producer Stephen Bochco. "The truth is, you fail at more things than you succeed at." Mr. Bochco should know. Along with creating the award-winning series "Hill Street Blues" and "L.A. Law," he's also been responsible for some less stellar efforts—like "Paris," "Bay City Blues," and the musical series "Cop Rock."

Visit your local multi-plex and see if everything playing there is a "perfect" movie. Or listen to the latest CD by your favorite pop star. Is every song a "perfect" gem or are some tunes better than others? That's why there are "Greatest Hits" albums, because every effort *can't* be a hit. Not with music, not with movies, not with your latest short story or even that one-page memo you just sweated out.

As William Saroyan put it: "You write a hit play the same way you write a flop." All you can do is try your best, then try again—with the next project, and the one after that. Along the way, you'll develop technique, stamina and—if

you're lucky—the ability to make your next effort better than
the last.

❑

*All my life I've been working on the work—every canvas
a sentence or paragraph of it. Each picture is only an
approximation of what you want. That's the beauty of being
an artist; you can never make the absolute statement, but
the desire to do so as an approximation keeps you going.*
                                            —Robert Motherwell

❑

I start a book and I want to make it perfect, want it to turn every
color, want it to *be the world.* Ten pages in, I've already blown it,
limited it. Made it less, marred it. That's very discouraging. I hate
the book at that point. After a while I arrive at an accommodation:
well, it's not the ideal, it's not the perfect object I wanted to make,
but maybe—if I go ahead and finish it anyway—I can get it right
next time. Maybe I can have another chance."

—Joan Didion, from *Writers at Work: The Paris Review Interviews*

30

DON'T YOU NEED A LOT OF DISCIPLINE TO BE A WRITER?

In the beginning, you do need a lot of discipline—until you discover that you want to write, need to write, and that the work of writing is a lot easier than the work of *not* writing.

"Don't you think you're exaggerating just a bit?"

Not at all.

When you're writing, *you're* in control; no one can tell you what to do or how to do it. (Not even this book.) You're alone in your workshop, tinkering not with wood and nails, but words and ideas—building poems, stories and dialogue where people say and do what *you* want them to.

Wouldn't that be nice in real life?

❑

In my head I have a whole army of people asking to be let out and waiting for my orders.

—Anton Chekhov

When I sit and write, I am master of the world. For one brief moment, I am God. I create reality.

—Carlos Fuentes

❑

Interviewer: But don't you get lonely spending the whole day writing by yourself?

Playwright: Lonely? I've just spent all day listening to a room full of characters in some very interesting situations. When I finish writing for the day, I want to be *alone* for a while.

31

A PAGE A DAY KEEPS
THE WORRY AWAY

When you're first starting out, sitting at your desk for even a minute or two can be an overwhelming challenge. You're getting up to make coffee, water the plants, alphabetize your CD collection—anything you can think of that doesn't involve sitting down and having to write something.

What's needed is discipline: learning how to write when you don't feel like writing.

"When I am at work," wrote Vincent Van Gogh, "I feel an unlimited faith in art, and am sure I shall succeed, but in days of physical prostration I feel that faith diminishing, and a doubt overwhelms me which I try to conquer by setting to work again at once."

Conquer your worry about *not* writing by writing every day—either by counting the minutes or counting the pages.

COUNTING THE MINUTES

In this game, the goal is to sit and write for a specified number of minutes, each day increasing your limit.

For example, suppose you start out by writing five minutes your first day, deciding to *increase* your limit by five minutes a day. Doesn't sound like much, does it? Yet by the end of the week, you'll be writing thirty-five minutes a day; by the end of two weeks, more than an hour a day. Within a month, if you're diligent about it, you'll find yourself writing *two and a half hours a day.* Not bad considering that just a month ago five minutes was your personal best.

"I'm sorry, but starting with even *five* minutes sounds like way too much."

Okay, let's start with *one* minute your first day, increasing your daily goal not by five minutes, but by *one* minute a day.

By the end of a month, you're writing thirty minutes a day; after two months, an hour a day; after six months, three hours a day. Finally, by the end of the year you're writing *six hours a day*—all by sticking to your routine of adding just *one minute* a day.

"What's the catch?"

Who said there was a catch?

"There's got to be a catch. It *can't* be that easy."

Okay, sometimes you will find yourself with a severe case of "ants in the pants." In the beginning, just staying in your chair for a specified number of minutes is no easy task. Think of it like learning how to meditate: At first, your mind wants to go everywhere but into the meditative state. In writing, it's pretty much the same. But it's not just the mind, it's also the *behind* that starts to wander.

Years ago, trying to develop discipline, I remember how excruciating it could be to even sit at my desk for more than a few minutes at a time. But little by little I increased my stamina, until one day I looked up at the clock and, "Three *hours* have gone by? That's impossible. *This clock has to be wrong.*"

I actually got up, went to another clock, and it really *had* been three hours. In the months that followed, I repeated this routine any number of times. I just couldn't believe time could go by that fast.

Then again, there *are* those days when even half an hour seems like a lifetime.

COUNTING THE PAGES

In this game, the goal is to finish a specified number of pages a day, without increasing your limit each day. At least not for a while.

For example, suppose you're writing a short story. You might say to yourself, "I won't stop writing until I've written at least *one* page for the day." And when you're first starting out, a page a day is a very nice goal. But you have to be strict with yourself. You can't say you're finished until you make it to the end of the page.

Of course, there can be a real advantage to using the page-count method. Because as soon as you reach your goal, you can quit for the day—even if it only took you ten minutes. Who cares how long it took you? You wrote a page, or two pages, and that's that. You're free for the day. Go take yourself a guilt-free vacation.

A word of caution: Before you start imagining long days filled with joyous celebration ("I'm free! I'm free! And it only took ten minutes!") keep in mind that there can also be a real *disadvantage* to the page-count method. Remember: You're not allowed to quit for the day until you've reached your page goal—*even if it takes ten hours to write one measly page.* (And it can happen.)

SO WHICH METHOD SHOULD I USE?

Don't worry, I'm not going to say, "Whichever works best for you."

Start by counting the minutes, working yourself up to a couple of hours a day. Then, when it feels right, try to establish a personal page goal. Maybe a page a day, maybe two. But be sure to set a goal that's *realistic* for you—one you can accomplish without chaining yourself to the desk thirty hours a day.

The idea is that success breeds success; failure, only more failure. For example, if your goal is three pages a day and you keep winding up with only two pages, you're failing every day. (A few days of this self-torture and you're depressed, irritable and ready to quit.) But if your goal is two pages and you're *writing* two pages, you're succeeding every day—which makes it a lot more likely you'll return the next day and succeed again.

As a fortune cookie of mine once said: *To avoid being disappointed, minimize expectations.*

SAME TIME, SAME PLACE

Just as you might wake up each morning at the same time, or take the dogs for a walk at a certain hour, make writing part of your daily routine. Know that at a certain time each day you'll be sitting at your desk or the kitchen table, wherever it is you've chosen to work. Make it the same time and same place every day, *and don't let anything get in your way.*

If the telephone keeps ringing, disconnect it or turn on the answering machine; if visitors come knocking at your door, post a "No Visitors" sign; if your neighbor's TV comes seeping through the wall, drown it out with music; if it's too nice a day, pull down the shades; if your husband, wife, lover or children want you for anything other than a full-blown medical emergency, tell them simply but firmly: "This is my writing time. If you bother me again I will turn into a raging banshee and devour my young."

□

There is no possibility, in me at least, of saying "I'll do it if I feel like it."... I must get my words down every day whether they are any good or not.

—John Steinbeck

Work every day. No matter what has happened the day or night before, get up and bite on the nail.

—Ernest Hemingway

You have to sing every day so you can build up to being, you know, Amazingly Brilliant.

—Mick Jagger

❑

In 1958, George Plimpton, interviewing Ernest Hemingway for *The Paris Review*, noted: "He keeps track of his daily progress—'so as not to kid myself'—on a large chart made out of the side of a cardboard packing case and set up against the wall under the nose of a mounted gazelle head. The numbers on the chart showing the daily output of words differ from 450, 575, 462, 1250, back to 512, the higher figures on days Hemingway puts in extra work so he won't feel guilty spending the following days fishing on the Gulf Stream."

Figuring 250 words a page, most days Hemingway was writing about two pages a day. Not a huge output, but enough to add up to nine novels and about seventy short stories.

32

FIRST, DO A WARM-UP

Just as an athlete does various stretches to warm up before a game or match, writers warm up with their own kind of stretches—from lifting a coffee cup to their lips a hundred times or so, to various mental exercises.

This morning, for example, I wrote a letter to an out-of-town friend as a way to get my fingers and mind moving in the same direction. True, it would have been a lot easier to just make a phone call. But it would not have helped me to discover—as writing a letter always does—"Hey, I really *do* have something to say. Maybe I can lick today's work, after all."

Am I blowing my own horn here?
Maybe.
Is it getting me in gear for the day's work?
Absolutely.

From Sigmund Freud to Groucho Marx, the complete list of famous letter writers could probably fill a book, or at least this paragraph. For starters, consider: Michelangelo, Vincent Van Gogh, Thomas Jefferson, Ernest Hemingway, F. Scott Fitzgerald, John Steinbeck, Franz Kafka, Carl Jung, William James, Henry James, James Thurber, Flannery O'Connor, Henry Miller, Marcel Proust, Jack London, Virginia Woolf,

H. L. Mencken, Louis Anderson, Louis Armstrong (who signed his letters, "Red beans and ricely yours"), Walt Whitman, Charlie Weaver, Joseph Conrad, Anais Nin, Katherine Anne Porter, George Bernard Shaw, Rainer Maria Rilke, Jean-Paul Sartre, Simone de Beauvoir and the possible all-time record holder, with over 100,000 letters, Lewis Carroll.

❑

The proper definition of "Man" is an animal that writes letters.

—Lewis Carroll

❑

GIVE IT A TRY

Write a letter to an out-of-town friend and save on your phone bill; write a letter of protest to right a wrong—that'll get you going even better than caffeine; or write a letter to the son of your former governess:

My dear Noel,
I don't know what to write to you, so I shall tell you a story about four little rabbits, whose names were Flopsy, Mopsy, Cottontail and Peter.

That's how Beatrix Potter started out and she wound up with *Peter Rabbit*.

For a more contemporary example, consider Don Novello, ("Saturday Night Live"'s Father Guido Sarducci), who spends much of his time posing as Lazlo Toth, Citizen, writing super-patriotic, off-the-wall letters to famous people like Richard Nixon and H. R. Haldeman. Not only has he received lots of responses, he's published them (along with the letters that prompted them) as two volumes of *The Lazlo Letters*.

But here's the brilliant part: By printing his letters on the left-hand page and the responses on the right, Mr. Novello only has to write half the book, getting his famous respondents to write the other half. *And for free.*

A WORD OF ADVICE

When you do write a letter, keep a copy for yourself. After all, why go mailing off some of your best ideas and never get to see them again?

If you don't feel like writing a letter, try starting out by going over your work from the day before, making brief corrections and tidying things up. Working it over like this, you'll get back into the same mind-set—giving yourself a springboard for your next round of writing. *Be careful, though.* You're trying to keep writing, not get bogged down in wholesale editing.

33

IMITATION IS . . .
A VERY SMART IDEA

When I was eleven years old, I spent the summer writing letters to a friend in camp, the kind of funny, folksy letters humorist Charlie Weaver once published as a book. Actually, I found his book in the library one day and thought it was so good I decided to copy it—not "copy," exactly; I'd add a line or two, change some of the names so they were the same as some of the kids we both knew. But basically—yeah—I copied it. Along the way, I learned how to write.

That's how you get started, by imitating others. Whatever your artistic pursuit—writer, artist, performer, musician—it usually begins when you're so inspired by someone, you wish *your* work could be as good. In music, for example, Bob Dylan started out by imitating Woody Guthrie, Bruce Springsteen by imitating Dylan, and k. d. lang by sounding a lot like Patsy Cline. Keith Richards and Eric Clapton learned blues guitar from Robert Johnson records; Miles Davis said he learned to play ballads by listening to Coleman Hawkins; Dizzy Gillespie "learned rhythm patterns" from Charlie Parker; Elvis Presley borrowed from black rhythm-and-blues groups; and the Beatles borrowed from just about everyone, including Elvis Presley.

"A lot of things John and Paul did," recalls record producer George Martin, "were dead copies of things they'd heard. Paul's falsetto singing and the way they shook their heads was a takeoff of Little Richard. They would listen to American records, lift phrases, and work out how they'd want to do it. If George Harrison mastered a Chuck Berry riff, he would come home very proudly and play it ad nauseam."

In the world of movies, the story's the same. Just as Orson Welles learned to direct by watching John Ford's *Stagecoach*, Henry Jaglom got inspired to be a director by seeing Orson Welles's *Citizen Kane*. Likewise, Truffaut and DePalma were influenced by Hitchcock, and DePalma, it could be argued, has made a career out of imitating him.

Turn to comedy and the story doesn't change: Eddie Murphy learned from Richard Pryor; Richard Lewis learned from Woody Allen; and Woody Allen, according to biographer Eric Lax: ". . . learned the cadences of Bob Hope, the language of S. J. Perelman, the style of George Lewis, the outlook of Mort Sahl, the obsessions of Ingmar Bergman, the zaniness of the Marx Brothers, the soulfulness of Buster Keaton, the existential dilemma of Jean-Paul Sartre, the exaggerated exoticness of Federico Fellini, along with a score of additional influences, and (as they had built on others) he mixed their essences with his own to produce a unique sensibility."

The formula is simple:

INSPIRATION LEADS TO IMITATION, WHICH LEADS TO YOUR OWN STYLE.

Let the above examples be a lesson in liberation: If people like Bob Dylan and the Beatles can start by imitating others, so can you.

Borrow, imitate, steal from the best.

❑

Every musician, no matter who he is, hears something that clicks in him and [makes him think], "I'd sell my soul to be able to do that." That's how you become a musician. It's basic emulation to start with. You get through that and one day you realize, "Oh, I can do that." And then you start to live a bit and put your own stuff on it.

—Keith Richards

Jazz was never about arriving as an original.... You learn Coleman Hawkins or Ben Webster or John Coltrane and as time goes on you start to dissect your learning holistically and use the things you like and at that point you eventually sound like yourself.

—Branford Marsalis

❑

JUST BE CAREFUL:
BE INSPIRED BY OTHERS, NOT DEFEATED

"I could never write a song as good as 'Blowin' in the Wind,'" admits John Cougar Mellencamp. "Who am I kidding?" *This is where the amateur stops, packs up his pen and calls it a life. Or, as Mellencamp does, he continues with:* "...All I can really do is entertain myself, and hope along the way I can entertain somebody else." This is the difference between someone who demands perfection and accomplishes nothing, and someone who gives it up, and accomplishes everything.

Besides, what if you're wrong? What if you *could* write a song as good as "Blowin' in the Wind," but you "blow it" by not even trying?

FROM ERNEST HEMINGWAY TO YOU AND ME

Ernest Hemingway, when asked to name his influences, rattled off a list of thirty names, from Shakespeare to Chekhov, adding, "It would take a day to remember everyone." William Kennedy studied Faulkner; Raymond Carver learned from Chekhov; thousands of writers learned from Hemingway; and those writers (ranging from Joan Didion to Elmore Leonard) inspire others to write.

By reading others, we learn to write for ourselves. We read, as John Updike has said of himself, "not to come and judge, but to come and steal"—to sharpen our own skills.

☐

Originality is nothing but judicious imitation. The most original writers borrowed from one another. The instruction we find in books is like fire. We fetch it from our neighbors, kindle it at home, communicate it to others, and it becomes the property of all.

—Voltaire

Read, read, read. Read everything—trash, classics, good and bad, and see how they do it. Just like a carpenter who works as an apprentice and studies the master. Read! You'll absorb it. Then write. If it is good, you will find out. If it's not, throw it out the window.

—William Faulkner

☐

Writing Exercise:
Become a Typist for Your
"Favorite Author"

As a teenager, Joan Didion says she typed out Ernest Hemingway stories "to learn how the sentences worked. I taught myself to type at the same time." Gay Talese admired

F. Scott Fitzgerald's "Winter Dreams" so much, he typed it out to see what he could learn; and Mario Vargas Llosa recalls reading Faulkner "with a paper and pen, trying to decipher the structures."

Become a typist for your favorite author: Find a piece of writing you admire and copy it word for word.

"But that's so *boring*."

Not to Joan Didion and Gay Talese, it wasn't. And who sells more books, you or them?

Writing Exercise: "Steal That Style!"

"In the early books," says Robert B. Parker, "I made every effort to write just like Raymond Chandler. The degree to which those early books are different is the degree to which I failed in my attempt."

Having retyped someone's work, see how well you can imitate them on the page. Starting with a similar theme, or idea, try to write in the style of the person whose work you've just copied.

As an aspiring poet once wrote:

> and this is for nothing
> save the joy
> of having you
> this instant
> your fingers
> about my page.
>
> can you tell I've been reading
> e.e. cummings all day?

Remember: Don't expect to be 100 percent faithful—expect to be different. That's where *your* voice begins.

"I began assiduously examining the style and technique of those whom I once admired and worshipped: Nietzsche, Dostoievski, Hamsun, even Thomas Mann.... I imitated every style in the hope of finding the clue to the gnawing secret of how to write. Finally, I came to a dead end.... I began from scratch, throwing everything overboard, even those whom I most loved. Immediately I heard my own voice I was enchanted: the fact that it was a separate, distinct, unique voice sustained me. It didn't matter to me if what I wrote would be considered bad. Good and bad dropped out of my vocabulary.... My life itself became a work of art. I had found a voice, I was whole again."

—from *The Wisdom of the Heart,* by Henry Miller

❑

Writer Elmore Leonard says he was strongly influenced by Hemingway until he realized, "I didn't share his attitude about life. I didn't take myself so seriously." Taking himself less seriously, Leonard's gone on to write about twenty detective novels and make a pile of money.

34

THERE'S NOTHING NEW UNDER THE SUN

This book almost didn't get written because I was stupid enough to listen to someone in publishing who said: "Who needs another book about writing?"

Foolishly following this wrongheaded advice, I spent the next number of years *not* writing this book, convinced that I would be wasting my time with another "me too" book in an already crowded market. The years went on and I turned to other projects. I still wanted to write the book, but I kept coming back to that nagging question: "Who needs another book about writing?"

Clearly, this had been a rhetorical question, no answer needed or requested. But if nothing else I wanted to answer it for myself.

"Who needs another book about writing?"

I did.

I needed to write this book for myself—to see if I could take what I had learned over the years and write about it *my* way, with *my* particular slant on things. Because that's what was going to make my book different and, hopefully worth reading.

Like the Bible says: "[T]here is no new thing under the sun." All you can do is take something that's already been worked over (perhaps dozens of times) and try to make your version different, and therefore new.

Remember the movie *Ghost* (1990), where Patrick Swayze plays the ghost of Demi Moore's husband? Hailed as "fresh" and "original," what no one mentioned was that *Ghost* followed a long tradition of similarly themed films—from *The Ghost and Mrs. Muir* (1947) to *Kiss Me Goodbye* (1982), where Jeff Bridges plays the ghost of Sally Field's husband. Sound familiar?

Without a doubt, Bruce Joel Rubin, the writer of *Ghost*, knew that his script would not be without its predecessors. But what Rubin did was take a well-trodden story area and tell it *his* way, with his particular slant on things.

Take *Thelma and Louise* (1991). If you wanted to, you could easily dismiss it as "just another buddy film"—a road movie that happens to star women instead of men. You might even say it's a female version of *Butch Cassidy and the Sundance Kid* (1967). Yet, according to Janet Maslin in the *New York Times*, writer Callie Khouri "reinvents the buddy film with such freshness and vigor that the genre seems positively new."

Finally, consider "Every Breath I Take," one of the most successful songs written by Sting. You could say it's "an aggregate of every rock song ever written with a relative minor chord," as Sting himself has said, adding, "There's nothing original in it, not one thing. And yet it *is* original."

"You mean I don't have to be 100 percent original?"

Name one person who is.

Remember: There's nothing new under the sun. So don't let an old idea stand in your way, not for a second. Don't sit around waiting for the Big Idea; start with a small idea (like "two women go on a road trip") and *make* it big.

❑

If you are a maker, you will know that somewhere the thing you would do has already been done, and you will set about quietly to do it.

—Kenneth Patchen

Just do it.

—Nike commercial

❑

In 1958, Sidney Poitier made a movie called *The Defiant Ones*, about a black convict (Poitier) and his white accomplice (Tony Curtis), who are shackled together as they flee from the police in the rural South. Thirty years later, in 1988, Sidney Poitier made *Shoot to Kill*, about a black FBI agent (Poitier) and a white mountain man (Tom Berenger), who, through their mutual need, are "shackled" together to pursue a convict through the rural Northwest.

Screenwriter Harv Zimmel, who wrote *Shoot to Kill*, explained: "It wasn't my intent to ape *The Defiant Ones*, but Sidney saw the similarities and that drew him to the project."

How many different stories are there?

According to Georges Polti's classic work *The Thirty-Six Dramatic Situations*, all fiction and drama is based on thirty-six basic plots. Period.

Nothing new in your latest story, song, novel or screenplay? Don't worry about it.

35

STUMPED?

It's an embarrassing story, but it illustrates an important point: I was about seventeen when I was driving my mother's car and heard a *thump, thump, thump*. I got out, saw that I had a flat and started walking away.

Where was I going? I had no idea. All I knew was that the car didn't work anymore, so I was abandoning it. Half a block later, remembering there was a spare in the trunk, I had a brainstorm: "I may be stuck now," I thought, "but if I go back and change the tire, I can be on my way."

This is the difference between getting stuck and *abandoning* your writing, and finding a solution so you can *continue* writing.

Imagine you're about to leave the house when you can't find your car keys. Do you just give up, deciding it's not worth the effort? Or do you turn the house upside down until you find them? *Stop abandoning your writing at the first sign of trouble*. Writers get stuck just like tires go flat and keys get misplaced:

BEING STUMPED IS PART OF THE PROCESS.

Don't sit there beating yourself up about it. Work at it for a while, then take a break; go for a walk. Isaac Bashevis

Singer would walk more than a hundred blocks a day, working out his stories in his head. Going for a walk removes you from the pages, giving you a certain distance from your work. Take a long enough walk and either your feet give out or you come up with a breakthrough, like: "Hey, what about that spare in the trunk!"

"Any momentary change stimulates a fresh burst of energy," says Woody Allen. "This may sound silly, but I'll be working and I'll want to get into the shower for a creative stint.... I'll stand there in the steaming water for thirty or forty minutes, just plotting a story and thinking out ideas." For Irving Stone, it was moving into the garden, pulling weeds to clear his mind; for myself, living in New York, it was moving to the terrace, settling down in my Adirondack chair for a needed change of scenery.

A MINOR DISCOVERY

Over the years, I discovered that if I went out to the terrace with a pad and pencil, I hardly ever came up with a solution to whatever problem I'd gone there to solve; but if I walked out to the terrace *without* a pad and pencil, invariably I'd find the solution. Then I'd race back inside and write it down before I forgot it. It was as if I had tricked my mind into thinking it was on vacation. Once on vacation, it seemed, my mind could "unwind" enough to reveal certain insights.

Einstein said he often got his best ideas while shaving—before his mind started "working" for the day.

Let your problem go for a while and the answer may just come to you.

STILL STUMPED? GO TELL A FRIEND JUST HOW STUMPED YOU ARE

Sometimes, just explaining the problem to a friend can get you unstuck. It's like bringing another brain into the project—even if they don't say a word.

Next time you're having trouble at the typewriter, try popping into the office next door or calling a friend on the phone. Exchange a brief pleasantry or two, then jump right in: "You gotta help me, I'm going in circles with this thing. I'm trying to get across a pretty basic idea to my salespeople, but the more I write the more frustrated I get. What the hell's the matter here? Why can't I just write something like, *'Don't take "Just browsing" for an answer'*?"

See how much help even a "silent partner" can be?

Meanwhile, don't be concerned if the person you're talking to isn't familiar with a particular subject, or what you're trying to accomplish, exactly. The less they know, the more you'll be forced to make your presentation so simple, so clear, even *you'll* be able to figure it out.

❑

At its best, the sensation of writing is that of any unmerited grace. It is handed to you, but only if you look for it. You search, you break your heart, your back, your brain, and then—and only then—is it handed to you.

—*Annie Dillard*

❑

Writing Exercise: "Talk" Out Your Problem

Let's say you went for a walk, pulled some weeds, took a shower, called up some friends and you're *still* stumped. Now what?

Take a fresh sheet of paper and "talk" out your problem like you would with a friend. (Only this way, they can't hang up on you or tell you they've got more important things to do.) "Talking" on paper, come up with as many solutions as possible. *And don't edit yourself.* Whatever comes to mind, write it down.

Remember:

> "Blah, blah, blah. Blah, blah, blah.
> Blah, blah, blah . . . GOLD!"

"Sometimes when I was starting a new story and I could not get it going, I would sit in front of the fire and squeeze the peel of the little oranges into the edge of the flame and watch the sputter of blue that they made. I would stand and look out over the roofs of Paris and think, 'Do not worry. You have always written before and you will write now. All you have to do is write one true sentence. Write the truest sentence that you know.' So finally I would write one true sentence, and then go on from there. It was easy then because there was always one true sentence that I knew or had seen or had heard somebody say."

—from *A Moveable Feast,* by Ernest Hemingway

36

WRITER'S BLOCK
(CHIPPING AWAY AT IT)

There is no such thing as writer's block. (Thought that might get your attention.)

What you call writer's block I call *perfectionist's block*. Instead of sitting down and writing something, you worry that your work won't be good enough, or "perfect" enough; or you *start* writing something, but soon give up, convinced it's never going to be the "masterpiece" you'd imagined. One student I know spends 10 percent of his time writing and *90 percent* of the time worrying if his work is any good. He doesn't write very much, but he has plenty of time for worrying.

WHAT'S NEEDED IS COURAGE: HAVING THE FEAR BUT DOING IT ANYWAY

In *Butch Cassidy and the Sundance Kid*, there's a famous scene where Butch and Sundance chase up a mountain to avoid the relentless posse, only to find themselves at a dead end. The only way out, says Butch, is to jump a hundred feet or so to the fast-moving stream below. But Sundance won't hear of it.

> *BUTCH*
> It's the only way. Otherwise we're dead.

They argue about it for a while until Sundance admits the real reason for his obstinacy.

> *SUNDANCE*
> I can't swim.

> *BUTCH*
> You stupid fool, the fall'll probably kill you.

Finally, joining hands to take a literal leap of faith, they step off the cliff, yelling, "Sh-i-i-i-t!" as they free-fall to the stream below. They splash down and the current carries them along, swirling them to safety and more adventures in the days to come.

The choice is yours: You can sit home and watch old movies, or have your own adventure right on the page. All it takes is a "leap of faith"—writing in *spite* of the fear, even if you don't know how to swim.

HOW DO YOU FIND THE COURAGE TO WRITE WHEN YOU CAN'T FIND THE COURAGE TO WRITE?

You write.

You write knowing full well it's *not* going to be perfect, it's *not* going to be the best thing anyone ever wrote and you're *not* going to die facedown in a ditch because you just dared to write something that may not win the Nobel Prize.

Perfectionism?

Give it up.

High standards?

Lower them.

Afraid to take that leap of faith?
Face it. Fear it. Do it anyway.

◻

Walking the wire is life. Everything else is waiting around.
—Karl Wallenda, of The Flying Wallendas

◻

PUT IT AWAY, IF YOU MUST, BUT YOU MUST NOT GIVE UP

Filmmakers Joel and Ethan Coen, while writing the script for *Miller's Crossing*, found themselves with a severe case of writer's block. Putting the script aside, they started another one, *Barton Fink*, about a writer with a severe case of writer's block. Having completed *Barton Fink*, they went back and finished *Miller's Crossing*.

Neil Simon wrote thirty-five pages of *Brighton Beach Memoirs*, then put it away for nine years because "the wheels of inspiration had grinded to a halt." Meanwhile, he worked on other projects, writing about a play a year. Eventually, he returned to *Brighton Beach*, finished it and won the New York Drama Critics Award.

◻

The way to resume is to resume. It is the only way. To resume.

—Gertrude Stein

You must go on, I can't go on, I'll go on.
—Samuel Beckett, The Unnamable

◻

"I wrote at times without belief that I would ever finish, with nothing in me but black despair, and yet I wrote and wrote and could not give up writing. And it seemed that despair itself was the very goad that urged me on, that made me write even when I had no belief that I would ever finish."

—from *The Story of a Novel,* by Thomas Wolfe

37

WRITING AS THERAPY? YOU BET YOUR LIFE!

According to Dr. Edward J. Murray, a professor of psychology at the University of Miami, a study he conducted indicates that writing about emotional experiences "seems to produce as much therapeutic benefit as sessions with a psychotherapist." And it's a lot cheaper.

Frankly, I'm glad to hear that the science of psychology has finally caught up with what writers have known forever—writing makes you feel better. Allen Ginsberg once called imagination "the escape hatch." Anne Sexton began writing poems at the suggestion of her psychiatrist. And novelist Amy Tan, though she tried psychotherapy, says her psychiatrist fell asleep on her. "I felt so boring," said Tan. "But I decided that instead of seeing him I'd start writing fiction."

Like therapy, writing helps to organize your thoughts and feelings, lending order and structure to otherwise chaotic events; and fiction—because it *shapes* reality—can take those events and give them a purpose and meaning they may not actually have.

Instead of psychoanalysis (the "talking cure") take the " 'talking' on paper" cure and see where it leads. You might wind up with a best-selling novel (Amy Tan), win a Pulitzer Prize (Anne Sexton) or just plain amuse yourself enough to feel a little less boring.

Remember: Writing is one of the most fulfilling things you can do in life. It can fill your life with meaning, purpose and tremendous joy. But if you don't write—and you're driven to write—it will drain you mercilessly, like no other force on earth.

❑

Writing is a form of therapy; sometimes I wonder how all those who do not write, compose or paint can manage to escape the madness, the melancholia, the panic fear which is inherent in the human situation.

—Graham Greene

When I'm not writing, I'm dying.

—Neil Diamond

❑

"Once at a literary meeting I heard someone ask John Cheever why he wrote. He replied without hesitation, 'To try to make sense of my life.' That is the best answer I can conceive of. The life we all live is amateurish and accidental; it begins in accident and proceeds by trial and error toward dubious ends. That is the law of nature. But the dream of man will not accept what nature hands us. We have to tinker with it, trying to give it purpose, direction and meaning. . . ."

—from *Where the Bluebird Sings to the Lemonade Springs: Living and Writing in the West*, by Wallace Stegner

38

CHANCES ARE YOU'LL WRITE SOMETHING PRETTY GOOD

There's a theory that if a chimpanzee sat at a typewriter and kept hitting keys, he'd eventually produce the collected works of William Shakespeare, though he would have to sit there a very long time.

Same goes for your own writing—the more you write, the more time you spend at it—the better your chances for success.

Years ago, I was at a museum in Paris where one of the exhibition rooms was devoted to about twenty paintings of flowers in a vase. Variations on a theme, they were all by the same artist. Ten paintings on one wall, ten on the other. To me, they were strictly run-of-the-mill, the sort of thing you'd find at an outdoor art show. "What's the point," I thought, "why did they even bother to hang them up?" About to turn around and head somewhere else, I suddenly noticed—at the far end of the room—a huge, bright, *spectacular* painting of flowers in a vase. So that was the point:

IT MIGHT TAKE A FEW WHACKS AT IT
TILL YOU GET SOMETHING GOOD.

Consider the professional photographer who keeps snapping photos of his model for the next cover of *Vogue*, taking a hundred or more pictures to wind up with a single photograph worthy of the cover. Photographers call this "burning film," knowing that the more photos they take, the better their chances of getting a good one.

Keep in mind: Playing the game *this* way is the exact opposite of the perfectionist's point of view. You might say it's the difference between "Strike one, I'm out" and "Strike seventeen, I'm still up at bat!"

□

In the production of any genius, great painter or great artist, there are really only four or five things that really count in his life. The rest is just everyday filler.
—Marcel Duchamp

A good poet is someone who manages, in a lifetime of thunderstorms, to be struck by lightning five or six times. A dozen or two dozen times and he is great.
—Randall Jarrell

If you want to be a famous writer, keep at it for ten years. By that time everyone else will have quit and they'll have to hire you.
—Hollywood legend

□

39

CRITICISM

"No passion in the world," wrote H. G. Wells, "is equal to the passion to alter someone else's draft." Not everyone knows how to write, you'll discover, but everyone knows how to *rewrite*. My cousin Richard has worked as a pharmacist for the past twenty years. His hobby is collecting unusual doorknobs. Last week he called me and said: "I hear you're working on a book. Why don't you send me some chapters and I'll show you how to fix them."

Criticism isn't the tough part; it's how you react to it.

One day, while making my way down New York's Fifth Avenue, a crazy lady suddenly lunged at me, yelling: "It's all your fault!" Then she stormed off and I stood there for a full thirty seconds or so, thinking, "Maybe she's right, maybe it *is* all my fault." This is how vulnerable you can be to criticism—even when it's from a crazy person.

When it comes to your writing, try to keep things in perspective:

DON'T TAKE IT PERSONALLY.

People aren't criticizing you, they're criticizing something you wrote. They're not saying, "*You* need work"; they're saying, "What you *wrote* needs work." Think of it as the difference between, "I don't like you" and "I don't like your sweater." One you can change, the other you're stuck with.

TRUE STORY

A writer I know tells the following story: "I'm waiting for feedback on my latest screenplay when the phone rings and it's my friend Bobby, a screenwriter, who says: 'I have never met two characters who were *less* sympathetic; I didn't care if they lived or died.' I hang up the phone, devastated. Less than a minute later, the phone rings again. It's Brian, another writer friend, who tells me: 'I have never met two characters who were *more* sympathetic.'"

The moral of the story?

Opinions will vary. Sometimes quite wildly. Whether it's glowing praise or complete damnation, learn to shrug off either extreme. Praise will stop you from growing, scorn from even trying.

EVERYONE GETS A VOTE BUT YOU GET TO COUNT THEM

A couple of years ago, I ordered a rubber stamp from my local stationery store. Now, before I hand out a work in progress, I stamp on the front page:

THIS IS A ROUGH DRAFT ONLY!
All comments, criticisms and suggestions will be greatly appreciated—unless I don't agree with you, of course, in which case your vote doesn't count.

How do you decide what to listen to and what to ignore? You sift through everyone's comments and try to figure out what seems right to you, though if you hand your work to four or five people and they all say the same thing, there's a good chance they're on to something. I'm not saying to go with the majority, necessarily, but if a consensus seems to emerge, at least give it some thought.

Meanwhile, unless you're a Zen master, your knee-jerk reaction will usually be defensive. "What do you mean, you don't like what I wrote? What do *you* know, anyway?" What does your Aunt Millie know about writing short stories? Probably not that much. But she may like to read them. So if something about *your* story doesn't quite sit right with her, maybe her criticism has some merit, after all.

There's an old story about a Japanese poet who'd write a batch of poems, then go up to the mountains to read them to a peasant woman he knew. If she was confused by something, or didn't understand, the poet would make careful note of it. Then he'd go back home and try to rework them—or not.

The decision is yours. You can listen to your Aunt Millie and change things to suit her, or learn to smile and say, "Thanks for your comments, Aunt Millie, I'll take them under advisement."

Remember: Everyone gets a vote, but you get to count them.

❑

Ordinarily, if I show [my husband] a poem, something I try not to do, he says, "I don't think that's too hotsy-totsy," which puts me off. I try not to do it too often. My in-laws don't approve of the poems at all.

—Anne Sexton

I get letters like: 'The first act was my life but the second act wasn't my life.' Well, write your own play. Leave me alone.

—Wendy Wasserstein

I get terrible reviews everywhere I go. I don't read most of them, but I hear they are pretty stinkeroo, which is cool, because I'm not doing it for the critics. I'm doing it for myself and for the people who come to see me.

—Harry Connick, Jr.

❑

RANDY NEWMAN FAILS TO EXCITE CRITIC

Reading the *Los Angeles Times* this morning, I came across a concert review with the headline: RANDY NEWMAN FAILS TO EXCITE FANS. "There wasn't much liveliness in the room," wrote critic Richard Cromelin, "and even Newman seemed to sense the antiseptic atmosphere."

Well, I was at that concert. It wasn't "antiseptic"; it was cozy and intimate. As for the lack of "liveliness in the room," the evening ended with three standing ovations. I don't know about Mr. Cromelin, but to me that's pretty lively.

Poor Randy. He's probably moping around the house wondering what went wrong. That's why I wrote to him first thing this morning, setting the record straight and assuring him he did no wrong. (Also, it was a great warm-up for the day's writing.)

Like I said: *Opinions will vary.*

40

SELF-CRITICISM

More powerful than anyone else's criticism is *self*-criticism—the ability to zero in on your fragile psyche and beat yourself to a pulp with ruthless dedication.

"You mean, I shouldn't be critical of what I write?"

BE CRITICAL OF WHAT YOU WRITE, NOT THE PERSON WHO WROTE IT.

There's nothing wrong with looking at your work and saying, "I could do better." A critical eye will keep you on the alert, encouraging you to keep making progress. But when cool-headed criticism gets out of hand, it snakes around and aims for the *self*, twisting "I could do better" into "This is no good…I'm no good…Who am I trying to kid here, anyway?"

And how much of that can even the best of us take?

Instead, learn that bringing a healthy dose of criticism to your work will always serve you well. Just make sure it's a *healthy* dose, not a lethal one.

Remember: Be critical of what you write, not the person who wrote it.

❑

No artist is pleased. [There is] no satisfaction whatever at any time. There is only a queer dissatisfaction, a blessed unrest that keeps us marching and makes us more alive than the others.

—Martha Graham

□

While working on his novel, the writer confessed in his journal: "No one else knows my lack of ability the way I do.... My work is no good.... I'm desperately upset about it.... It isn't the great book I had hoped it would be. It's just a run-of-the-mill book. And the awful thing is that it is absolutely the best I can do."

The writer was John Steinbeck, writing about his novel *The Grapes of Wrath*.

41

DO IT YOUR WAY

You might think I'm crazy to say this, but here goes:

I CAN WRITE BETTER THAN ERNEST HEMINGWAY.

And not just because he's dead; because what I do is write *Saltzman's* way, just as Hemingway wrote his way. This is why Saltzman can write better than Hemingway, and Hemingway—even if he is dead—can write better than Saltzman. "One learns who one is," writes John Barth, "and it is at one's peril that one attempts to become someone else."

This book, for example, could not have been a serious, academic tome if my life depended on it. Instead, like Frank Sinatra, "I did it my way." Doing it *your* way, you'll learn, is not so much a choice as the only way that makes any sense.

Art Spiegelman wanted to write about his parents, survivors of the Holocaust. Deciding to present the story in a rather unusual format, he has his own character remark: "I feel so inadequate trying to reconstruct a reality that was worse than my darkest dreams. And trying to do it as a **comic strip**! I guess I bit off more than I can chew. Maybe I ought to forget the whole thing."

A cartoonist by trade, Spiegelman kept at it, writing the story over a thirteen-year span, with the Jews drawn as mice and the Nazis as cats. Published in 1987, *Maus: A Survivor's Tale* has been translated into sixteen languages, was nominated for a National Book Critics Circle Award and led to a second volume, *Maus II*, published in 1991. Doing it his way—writing in a way that made sense to him—Spiegelman wound up with the Pulitzer Prize.

In 1963, a young man named Christo wrapped a single magazine in plastic, twine and Scotch tape and called it art. From there, he went on to wrap the Museum of Contemporary Art in Chicago with 10,000 square feet of heavy tarp; run a twenty-four-and-a-half-mile long fence across fifty-nine ranches in northern California; surround eleven islands in Miami's Biscayne Bay with six million square feet of pink plastic; wrap the 400-year-old Pont-Neuf in Paris with 440,000 square feet of fabric; and erect 1,340 giant umbrellas in Japan and 1,760 more in California's Tejon Pass, sixty miles north of Los Angeles.

To realize these visions, Christo enlists hundred of helpers, all of whom work for free. Why all the eager help? Maybe it's because people get so excited by something daring for a change, they can't help but want to join in the act.

Like Spiegelman, Christo gets an idea and runs with it, doing it *his* way no matter how crazy or impossible it may seem. This is your job as a writer—to do it *your* way no matter how many voices seem to say, "My God, you can't do that!"

Sure you can. All you have to do is take the plunge.

❑

I say, play your own way. Don't play what the public want—you play what you want and let the public pick up on what you doing—even if it does take them fifteen, twenty years."
—**Thelonius Monk**

Everything I've ever been punished for, expelled for or hit for is what I get paid for today.

—**Howie Mandel**

❑

Singer Jay Hawkins started his music career studying opera, moving to jazz and then to blues. But there was nothing distinctive about his act until a record executive suggested he stop singing—and start screaming. And that's what turned Jay Hawkins into Screamin' Jay Hawkins, shrieking out songs like his fifties hit "I Put a Spell on You."

"I didn't have the best voice for blues and R&B," he says. "But I could scream. I called on my opera training. I can scream soprano—like a woman."

Talk about finding your *own* voice, I'd say he found it.

42

DON'T BE SHY

In the average workday, we spend most of our time being conservative, considerate and borderline boring. We keep a constant eye on our behavior and try our best not to ruffle feathers. But when you're writing, it's a whole other game—time to kick back, get out of your work clothes and let it rip.

Jazz saxophonist Stan Getz used to say: "I never played a note I didn't mean." We hear those words and we are in *awe* of their power. Would that we could say the same:

"I NEVER WROTE A WORD I DIDN'T MEAN."

Write it, mean it and don't change a thing for anyone but yourself. Writing is your turn to tell it like it is, letting the naysayers say what they may. And if you ruffle some feathers, *all the better.*

Think of writing as a circus act. Which would you prefer to watch—a high-wire aerialist without a net, or a low-wire act with a net? The one full of daring, or the one full of safety? The one that resists the limits, or the one that succumbs?

❑

There are four qualities essential to a great jazzman. They are taste, courage, individuality and irreverence.
—Stan Getz

That which is not daring is nothing.

—*Kenneth Patchen*

❑

A woman I know found herself in an elevator with Jack Nicholson. Noticing a quarter on the floor, they glanced at each other but neither made a move. Finally, Nicholson bent down, picked up the quarter and grinned, "The rich kid just got richer!"

The moral of the story?

Don't be shy.

❑

I got older, I got bolder.

—*Little Richard*

43

IN SEARCH OF INSPIRATION

I don't want to write today; I don't feel inspired. I didn't feel inspired yesterday and I may not feel inspired tomorrow. I'd much prefer to wait until I do feel inspired—which could be tomorrow, or a week from next Thursday. Not knowing when I will feel inspired, there's only one thing to do: get to work and *get* inspired.

There's nothing magical about inspiration. It doesn't come from chanting, burning incense or watching the sunset; it comes from work and discipline, sitting at your desk and *making* it happen.[1] Writer and adventurer Jack London said it best:

"YOU CAN'T WAIT FOR INSPIRATION. YOU HAVE TO GO AFTER IT WITH A CLUB."

If you sit around waiting for inspiration, that's just what you'll do—sit around waiting for inspiration.

What about the accountant who doesn't feel like adding up numbers today? Or the surgeon who's just not in the mood to remove your appendix? Writers do not have the

---

[1]Don't get me wrong: There's nothing wrong with meditation, incense, chanting, channeling or anything else that gets you in the mood. Just don't confuse getting in the mood with getting the work done.

market on feeling uninspired. If you're a writer, you write. That's your job.

TRUE STORY

This morning, I awoke to crisp, cool air, a burst of sunshine and the smell of dog poop on the living-room carpet. Both dogs, black Labrador retrievers, had decided to leave their mark on a carpet that was barely a week old. Cleaning up their mess, I worked myself into a tizzy.

"That's it. Forget about writing today. Call it off. Forget the whole thing!"

What had started out as a perfect morning was now a rotten day begging to be blown off. After coffee and a shower, on the verge of going out for breakfast and not coming back, I forced myself to sit down and work.

I grumbled for a while, then found my inspiration: I wrote out this story and immediately felt better.

Six hours later—having cranked out four more pages—I felt even better.

Remember: If you don't feel like writing, tough shit.

❑

I don't try to be inspired; I just try to work very regularly. . . . I think most artists feel that being inspired is a myth. Simply put, out of the work, comes the work.

—John Cage

I have forced myself to begin writing when I've been utterly exhausted, when I've felt my soul as thin as a playing card, when nothing has seemed worth enduring for another five minutes . . . and somehow the activity of writing changes everything. Or appears to do so.

—Joyce Carol Oates

❑

"I always have a clock in front of me. Sometimes, if things are going badly, I will force myself to write a page in a half an hour. I find that can be done. I find what I write when I force myself is generally just as good as what I write when I'm feeling inspired. It's mainly a matter of forcing yourself to write."

—Tom Wolfe, from *Writers at Work: The Paris Review Interviews*

44

SCRAPS AND OVERHEARDS: GRAB THAT IDEA

In Chapter 5 I mentioned being at a party and coming up with the expression: "If you can talk, you can write." Knowing a good phrase when I hear one, I immediately grabbed a cocktail napkin and wrote it down. Had I not written those words down, not only would I have forgotten them by morning, you would not be reading this book today.

WORDS FALL FROM OUR MOUTHS AND EVAPORATE. WRITE THEM DOWN AND THEY STAY FOREVER.

Much of this book, in fact, comes from various things that have "fallen from my mouth," either in class or in conversations with students—things I had the good sense to immediately write down: on scraps of paper, receipts, the backs of business cards, anything that was handy. This is a true example of the "Blah, blah, blah, GOLD" theory of writing: *If you keep talking long enough, you'll say something interesting*.

Whether it's things you say, hear other people say, read or observe, or things that just come to mind, if something strikes your fancy, make a note of it; write it down; save it before it *evaporates* and you can't for the life of you remember that great idea you had just a minute ago. Or that so-so idea you could have made into a great one—*if you could only remember the damn thing.*

Good ideas are like radio waves; they're all around us, there for the grabbing. All you have to do is tune them in. As creative consultant Roger von Oech advises in *A Whack on the Side of the Head*: "Develop the hunter's attitude, the outlook that wherever you go, there are ideas waiting to be discovered."

For myself, the hunt for ideas is a daily one, covering the widest terrain possible: newspapers from both coasts, magazines I subscribe to (plus ones I read on the stand), books, films, fortune cookies, songs on the radio, museums, conversations with auto mechanics, conversations with myself, a wild remark by a strange passerby ("It's all your fault!"). Every idea goes into the hopper, written down on scraps of whatever, then Scotch-taped or rewritten onto index cards.

Joseph Heller never leaves home without a small stash of three-by-five index cards tucked into his wallet. "If I think of a good sentence," he says, "I write it down."

When you get an idea, don't say to yourself, "I'll make a note of it when I have the time." Write it down the moment it occurs to you, before you forget it. At the end of the day, empty out your pockets and lay out your scraps. Then you can decide what to keep and what to toss. At least the decision will be up to you, not up to your memory.

Got an idea?

Grab it.

Don't let a good idea get away.

❑

When I'm not writing, sometimes I hear or see things and consciously think, "I ought to remember that, that may come in handy sometime." And then the next instant it's gone. But when I'm in the obsessive stage, I'm a sponge.
—**William Goldman**

The artist is a receptacle for emotions that come from all over the place: from the sky, from the earth, from a scrap of paper, from a passing shape, from a spider's web. . . . We must pick out what is good for us where we can find it.

—*Pablo Picasso*

❑

When Woody Allen was appearing as a stand-up comedian, his entire act was made from scraps.

"[The material was] constructed from ideas and lines he jotted down on scraps of napkins, bits of paper, and backs of matchbook covers as they came to him and then tossed in a drawer. When he worked on the act, he laid the litter out on the floor of his apartment and walked around in it like a gardener in his vegetable patch, picking what was ripe. (When Norma Lee Clark, his secretary of twenty-five years, came to work for him, he brought her a suitcase full of paper scraps and asked her to type them out. They filled two hundred pages.)"

—from *Woody Allen: A Biography*, by Eric Lax

OVERHEARDS

What's an overheard? Something you heard that tickled your fancy. A bit of dialogue or a little scene you were smart enough to jot down and save for future use. Consider the following, collected over the past few months with very little effort:

• In a Los Angeles post office, a woman buying stamps shouts at the clerk: "I don't want anything with the word 'Love' on it!"

• In Boston's Little Italy, one produce vendor says to another: "He's been complaining about that for thirty years."

• In a Beverly Hills hair salon, the beautician tells her client: "He's crazy! She's sixteen years old and he wants to give her a nose job and cheek implants."

• Selling magazine subscriptions door to door, the salesman tells me he only gets 15 percent commission. "It's not much," he says, "but oatmeal's better than no meal."

• A woman tells her date that she ruined her car engine in 1968 when she ignored the oil light on her dashboard because she thought it was a "conspiracy by the oil companies to sell more oil."

Writing Exercise:
"Scavenger Hunt"

Raymond Carver said he once heard someone say, "That's the last Christmas you'll ever ruin for us!" Later, "using only that one line and other things I imagined, imagined so accurately that they *could* have happened, I made a story—'A Serious Talk.'"

During the week, be on the lookout for scraps or overheards. *And be sure to write them down.* At the end of the week, choose one idea and use "guided" freewriting to imagine the rest. (Or use one of the overheards above and get started right away.)

□

There are significant moments in everyone's day that can make literature. You have to be alert to them and pay attention to them. That's what you ought to write about.
—**Raymond Carver**

□

"I used to drive out to John's house," says Paul McCartney. "He lived out in the country, and I lived in London. I remember asking the chauffeur once if he was having a good week. He said, 'I'm very busy at the moment. I've been working eight days a week.' And I thought, 'Eight days a week! Now there's a title.'"

45

PRIVATE WRITING IN PUBLIC PLACES

Beethoven and Stravinsky scribbled music on napkins and menus; playwright August Wilson started out writing in bars and restaurants; Isaac Bashevis Singer wrote short stories in a pastry shop near his home; and there probably isn't an artist in the world who hasn't doodled on a napkin or wound up a meal wanting to frame his tablecloth.

Maybe it's the hum of people, a kind of white noise that clears your mind and helps you to concentrate, or the comfort of strangers who seem to say: "It's okay; you're not alone in the world." Working in public, writes David Mamet, "gives to the lone creator the satisfaction of fulfilling a place in society."

"This is who I am," you say. "I'm a writer."

❏

To write, I go every morning to the same café. . . . The fact that the café is crowded does not matter a bit. Whatever happens does not concern me. People can be talking very loudly beside me; I don't hear, I just concentrate.
—Nathalie Sarraute

❏

Writing Exercise:
"What's Their Relationship?"

Go to some public place and find a couple that interests you. Observing them the best you can (without getting caught), ask yourself: "What's their relationship?" Are they lovers? Ex-lovers? Dating? Divorcing? Have they known each other a long time or is this their first—and possibly last—time together?

TRUE STORY

It was spring and I was holding hands with my sister as we crossed the street. Crossing from the other direction, a young man spotted us and seemed to sigh, "If I could only be as in love as those two." He didn't know the facts, of course, but he made a whole story up—right on the spot.[1]

Now it's your turn: Find a couple that interests you and write out their story—regardless of what the facts might be.

[1] Then again, maybe I'm making *his* story up. What if he didn't envy us? What if he pitied us? What difference does it make? I got my story and that's all that counts.

46

BUT I DON'T HAVE TIME TO WRITE

"If I like writing so much," he complains, "why don't I do it more often?"

"I don't know, maybe you're lazy."

"But you don't understand, I have a full-time job."

"So did a lot of people."

Joseph Heller wrote *Catch-22* while working full-time writing advertising and promotion copy; Elmore Leonard was a copywriter for eleven years before his fiction writing earned him a living; and Oscar Hijuelos, before he won a Pulitzer Prize for *The Mambo Kings Play Songs of Love*, supported himself by working as a gofer at an advertising agency. James Dickey (also in advertising) wrote his first book of poems "on company time," and Wallace Stevens wrote his poems while working as a life insurance salesman. Joan Didion and Dorothy Parker started out at *Vogue*; Kurt Vonnegut, Jr., wrote short stories while working at General Electric; Henry Miller worked for Western Union; T. S. Eliot worked in a bank; Raymond Carver worked nights as a janitor; and Katherine Dunn wrote her first novel "while working three part-time jobs a day—proofreader for a printing house, invalid's companion, and Sugar Daddy wrapper at a Cambridge candy factory." (And don't forget Ben Hamper, riveter, and Mary Cahill, carpooler.)

When they first started out, none of these people had the time to write. But they *made* the time—early mornings, nights, weekends, days when they called in sick and probably weren't.

Consider Gerald Petievich, who took a night class in fiction writing while working as a detective for the United States Secret Service. For the next seven years he woke up at 4:00 A.M., getting a few hours of writing in before going to work. Hitting it big with his third pre-dawn novel, *To Live and Die in L.A.*, he quit the Secret Service in 1985, became a full-time writer and can't remember the last time he woke up at four in the morning.

Remember: If you want time to write, you find the time; if you want time to gripe, you sleep in and still have the time.

❑

I had to write from five to seven a.m. because the kids would get up and start running around. That went on for about eight years.

—Elmore Leonard

❑

John Grisham was a small-town criminal defense attorney who took out a legal pad and started writing a novel as a hobby. Writing in longhand, it took him three years to write *A Time to Kill*.

At the time of this writing, *A Time to Kill* is number three on the *New York Times* Paperback Best Sellers list, preceded only by *The Pelican Brief* and *The Firm*—both by Grisham.

Writing at night and on weekends, Benjamin Hoff wrote *The Tao of Pooh* while working full-time pruning trees. He wrote his next book, *The Te of Piglet*, while living off royalties from *The Tao of Pooh*.

47

GET REJECTED,
NOT DEJECTED

Aunt Bertha reads your latest work and gives you a nasty look.
"That's it, I'm finished as a writer."

One bad look and you're ready to quit? How many
books has Aunt Bertha written?

❑

A first-time novelist sends out his manuscript and gets 121
rejections. Sending it out *one more time*, Robert M. Pirsig gets
his first yes and *Zen and the Art of Motorcycle Maintenance* goes
on to sell more than three million copies.

❑

For nine years, a would-be country singer gets turned down
by every major recording label—*twice*. In 1985 he gets his big
break. Randy Traywick signs with Warner Brothers and
changes his name to Randy Travis.

❑

"I've been rejected thousands of times," says Warren Adler,
author of *The War of the Roses*. "And after every rejection I
say, 'What do they know?'"

Indeed. What did the experts know about Robert M.
Pirsig, Randy Travis or anyone else who's piled up a bunch

of no's before they got *one* yes and proved everyone wrong? *And you're still letting Aunt Bertha decide?*

In 1934, a reader at Warner Brothers Pictures made the following report about a script he'd reviewed: "I don't think you'd be missing anything to pass this up. I read quite a lot of it, and it's a draggy tale, unrelieved by either comedy or practical colorful incident.... I think we should leave this alone."

Fourteen years later, in 1948, John Huston's screenplay for *Treasure of Sierra Madre* won the Oscar for Best Screenplay.

48

PERSISTENCE

I was going over my taxes with Harry, the accountant, when he boorishly inquired: "That's all you made this year? What the hell are you doing with your life?"

"Well, I'm trying to make a living as a writer."

"That's what you were doing last year."

"And the year before and the year before that."

"You're not embarrassed by this? When are you going to give it up, already? Get a real job?"

Enough was enough. I leaned over the desk and looked him square in the eye. "Listen to me, you idiot. I'm going to hit it big one day and you're going to be the first person to go around bragging, '*I* knew him before he made it; *I* used to do his taxes.'"

Harry squirmed in his chair. "You're right."

"I know I'm right."

P.S.: Harry no longer does my taxes, though I will send him an autographed copy of this book, signed: See Chapter Forty-Eight: Persistence.

❑

Stick to it in spite of hell and other people. Patience and endurance.

—Katherine Anne Porter

❑

During World War II, a private in the U.S. Army tried his hand at writing poetry, sending a copy of a poem he'd written to his father. In turn, the father sent the poem to an editor at the *Syracuse Journal*, who advised in a letter, "Better the boy should be a butcher."

Undeterred, Private Rod Serling went on to become one of the most famous writers in television history, winning six Emmys and a Peabody Award, and creating the legendary series *The Twilight Zone*.

49

TALENT

"What if I don't have the talent?"
   What if you do?
   "What if I'm wasting my time?"
   What if you're *not* writing and wasting your time?

I was about seven years old when I discovered an old Royal typewriter in the basement. I rolled in some paper, hit a single letter and called upstairs: "Mom, do you have to hit the space bar after each letter or will the typewriter do it by itself?"

Immediately, my mother came back with the kindest, most nurturing answer possible: "Find out yourself!"

If you're wondering about talent, that's all you can do—start banging away and find out yourself. In time, you'll discover that good writing is not about magical aptitude or God-given gifts; it's about taking the talent you do have— great, average or less than average—and working hard to make the most of it.

   "But what if I have no talent whatsoever?"
   Work a little harder.

When a young actor named Arnold Strong made his film debut in *Hercules in New York* (1970), his performance was universally panned, and his English was so bad his dialogue had to be dubbed by someone else. Clearly, this was a talent *not* to be reckoned with—until Strong worked on his English, changed his name back to Schwarzenegger and said "Hasta la vista, baby" to the tag of no talent.

50

ADVICE

When people give you advice and say, "This is what I would do," they're right, it's what *they* would do.

Just remember: What you can do—better than anyone—is write it *your* way, no matter what they say.

❏

If I had to give young writers advice, I'd say don't listen to writers talking about writing.

—Lillian Hellman

Listen to Lillian.

—Joel Saltzman

❏

POP QUIZ #5

(Ten final questions you can't get wrong)

1. Conquer your fear about *not* writing by _____ every day.
   a) drinking
   b) drooling
   c) eating everything in sight
   d) writing

2. To develop good discipline, try counting the minutes or counting the _____.
   a) sheep
   b) sands of time
   c) noses on your face
   d) pages

3. Inspiration leads to imitation, which leads to _____.
   a) plagiarism
   b) voyeurism
   c) becoming an Elvis impersonator
   d) your own style

4. Don't sit around waiting for the _____; start with the small idea and *make* it big.
   a) perfect wave
   b) cable installer
   c) Big Kahuna
   d) Big Idea

5. What most people call writer's block, we call _____.
   a) hell
   b) constipation
   c) a house with no windows
   d) perfectionist's block

6. What's needed is courage: having the _____ but doing it anyway.
   a) willies
   b) heebie-jeebies
   c) good excuse
   d) fear

7. As Neil Diamond says: "When I'm not writing, I'm _____."
   a) out by the pool
   b) spending my money
   c) combing my hair
   d) dying

8. When it comes to criticism, everyone gets a vote but you get to _____.
   a) ignore them
   b) cry foul
   c) cry yourself a river
   d) count them

9. If you want time to write, you _____.
   a) quit your job
   b) set the clock back
   c) rob a bank, go to prison and get all the time you want
   d) find the time

10. If inspiration doesn't come to you, _____.
    a) go to sleep
    b) go to the movies
    c) don't be surprised
    d) go after it with a club

Answer Key: 1) d, 2) d, 3) d, 4) d, 5) d, 6) d, 7) d, 8) d, 9) d, 10) d

ONE LAST WORD

Write.